Woodworking
for the *Backyard*

Projects for Relaxing, Cooking, Entertaining & Gardening

SHADY OAK PRESS
MINNETONKA, MINNESOTA

Woodworking for the Backyard

Projects for Relaxing, Cooking, Entertaining & Gardening

CREDITS

Tom Carpenter
Creative Director

Dan Cary
Photo Production Coordinator

Chris Marshall
Editor, Editorial Coordinator

Steve Anderson
Assistant Editor

Richard Steven
Lead Project Designer, Copy Writer

Marti Naughton
Series Design, Art Direction & Production

Kim Bailey
Photographer

Tom Deveny, Jon Hegge, John Nadeau
Project Builders

Bruce Kieffer
Technical Illustrations

John Drigot
Contributing Project Designer

Brad Classon
Production Assistance

SHADY OAK PRESS

12301 Whitewater Drive
Minnetonka, MN 55343

1 2 3 4 5 6 / 12 11 10 09 08 07
ISBN: 978-1-58159-345-7
© 1999 North American Membership Group, Inc.

Distributed by:
Sterling Publishing Co., Inc.
387 Park Avenue South
New York, NY 10016-8810

For information about custom editions, special sales, premium and corporate purchases, please contact Sterling Special Sales Department at 800-805-5489 or specialsales@sterlingpub.com

Contents

Patio Table & Chairs (22)

Picnic Table & Benches (54)

Tiletop BBQ Center (30)

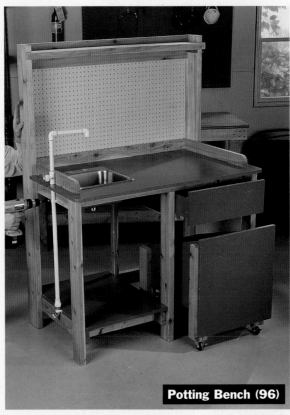
Potting Bench (96)

Basic Adirondack Chair (8)

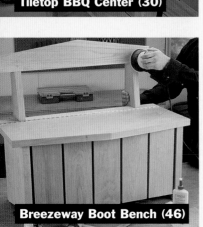
Breezeway Boot Bench (46)

Planters (88)

Sun Lounger (114)

Porch Glider (76)

Basic Garden Bench (140)

Frame-style Sandbox (40)

Daytripper Chair (62)

Advanced Adirondack Chair (14)

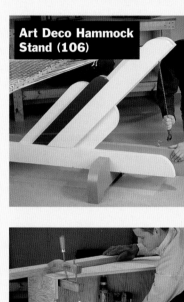
Art Deco Hammock Stand (106)

Daytripper Table (68)

Utility Cart (132)

Woven Wood Deck Chair (124)

Formal Garden Bench (148)

Introduction

Wood projects designed for outdoor use tend to be rugged and sturdy, utilizing simple joinery techniques and able to withstand extreme changes in temperature and humidity. Building outdoor projects can be a great way to develop and practice woodworking skills, while at the same time creating attractive pieces that you and your family will use for years to come.

In *Woodworking for the Backyard,* you'll find 18 outdoor projects that cover a diverse range of styles and levels of complexity. Some projects are quite basic, and well within the capability of all woodworkers; others are more refined, meant for sheltered spaces like porches and breezeways and requiring a higher level of woodworking skills for successful completion.

Each project includes a beautiful photograph of the finished piece, complete cutting and shopping lists, detailed plan drawings, clear color photographs of key points in the building process and straightforward step-by-step instructions. Before you dive right into making your first project, we encourage you to review the following two pages, where we've highlighted information that will provide a helpful introduction to choosing, joining and finishing wood for outdoor projects.

IMPORTANT NOTICE

For your safety, caution and good judgment should be used when following instructions described in this book. Take into consideration your level of skill and the safety precautions related to the tools and materials shown. Neither the publisher, Shady Oak Press, nor any of its affiliates can assume responsibility for any damage to property or persons as a result of the misuse of the information provided. Consult your local building department for information on permits, codes, regulations and laws that may apply to your project.

SUITABLE WOODS FOR OUTDOOR PROJECTS

Outdoor wood furniture can survive for many years in the elements, but the kind of wood you use will influence the longevity of your project. A number of wood species contain natural oils that make them more resistant to rotting, insect infestation and degradation from ultraviolet sunlight than other woods. Weather-resistant woods we use for projects featured in this book include Western red cedar, white oak and Honduras mahogany. Other excellent wood choices for outdoor projects include redwood, teak and cypress, but these varieties are harder to find in many areas of the United States and can be quite expensive.

Naturally weather-resistant woods include, from left to right, redwood, cedar, white oak and teak.

Wood products like treated lumber and exterior-grade plywood are also good options for outdoor projects, but you'll probably want to reserve these woods for projects you plan to paint. Treated lumber is pressure-infused with chemicals that make it insect- and moisture-resistant. Exterior-grade plywood is made with waterproof glue, so it resists delaminating when it comes into contact with moisture.

Other less weather-durable woods, like red oak and pine, can be used for outdoor projects as well, but these woods must be topcoated thoroughly with primer and paint or other UV protective sealers. It's a good idea to keep projects made from these woods in an area sheltered from moisture or direct ground contact and store them inside during seasons when they aren't in use.

STEP 1: Drill a counterbored pilot hole deep enough into the wood so the counterbored portion of the hole can accommodate both the screw head and a plug.

STEP 2: Drive the screw into the hole until it stops at the bottom of the counterbore. Glue and insert a wood plug cut from the same wood species or from a piece of dowel.

STEP 3: Trim any protruding portion of the wood plug flush with the surrounding wood using a flush-trimming handsaw. Then sand the plug area smooth.

COUNTERBORING & PLUGGING

One way to refine the look of outdoor furniture is to conceal screw heads with wood plugs. Wood plugs also keep galvanized screws sealed from moisture, which can otherwise cause them to react with woods like white oak and cedar over time, producing black stains. Counterboring and plugging are used on several projects in this book. To install wood plugs, drill pilot holes for the screws with a counterbore bit. The counterbore portion of the hole needs to be deep enough to fit both the countersunk screw head and the wood plug. Then bore wood plugs with a plug cutter in a drill press and cut them out with a band saw (See this technique on page 156). Glue and insert the plugs and sand smooth.

Wood preservatives with UV additives (left) are often sold as deck finishes and offer a couple years' worth of protection. Spar varnish (right) provides an even tougher moisture seal.

Exterior-grade latex primers and paints have come a long way in terms of durability, and they are easier to clean up than oil-based paints. Use primer with a stain blocker to seal woods like cedar that are prone to bleed oils through a painted finish.

CHOOSING AN OUTDOOR WOOD FINISH

It's a good idea to topcoat even weather-resistant woods as a final project step, especially if you want to retain the wood's natural color. Without a UV protective finish, woods like cedar and mahogany will turn a harmless silvery gray color, which may not achieve the look you're after for your project. Apply several coats of a clear or tinted penetrating water-repellent preservative with ultraviolet inhibitors and a mildewcide, or use marine-grade spar varnish, a favorite of boat builders. Plan to recoat annually for projects that are kept outside all the time. The other route to take for exterior finishes is to use a premium-quality latex primer followed by multiple coats of exterior latex paint.

Basic Adirondack Chair

No piece of outdoor furniture conjures up an image of elegance and rugged outdoor comfort quite like the Adirondack chair. There are many variations of this American classic. This design features a straightforward concept and easy-to-work materials for a satisfying project that can be built in a day, yet provide years of enjoyment.

Vital Statistics: Basic Adirondack Chair

TYPE: Adirondack chair

OVERALL SIZE: $36\frac{1}{2}$W by 37D by $37\frac{1}{2}$H

MATERIAL: Cedar

JOINERY: Butt joints reinforced with galvanized deck screws

CONSTRUCTION DETAILS:
· Largely square, straight cuts can be made with simple hand or power tools
· Chair made entirely from dimension lumber
· Exposed screws throughout to enhance rustic appearance

FINISHING OPTIONS: Penetrating UV protectant sealer, exterior paint or leave unfinished to weather naturally to gray

Building time

 PREPARING STOCK
0 hours

 LAYOUT
1-2 hours

 CUTTING PARTS
2-4 hours

 ASSEMBLY
2-4 hours

 FINISHING
2-4 hours

TOTAL: 7-14 hours

Tools you'll use

· Jig saw or circular saw
· Drill/driver
· Tape measure
· Combination square
· Clamps

Shopping list

☐ (4) 1 × 4 in. × 8 ft. cedar
☐ (2) 1 × 8 in. × 6 ft. cedar
☐ (1) 2 × 4 in. × 10 ft. cedar
☐ Galvanized deck screws ($1\frac{1}{4}$-, 2-in.)
☐ Finishing materials

Basic Adirondack Chair

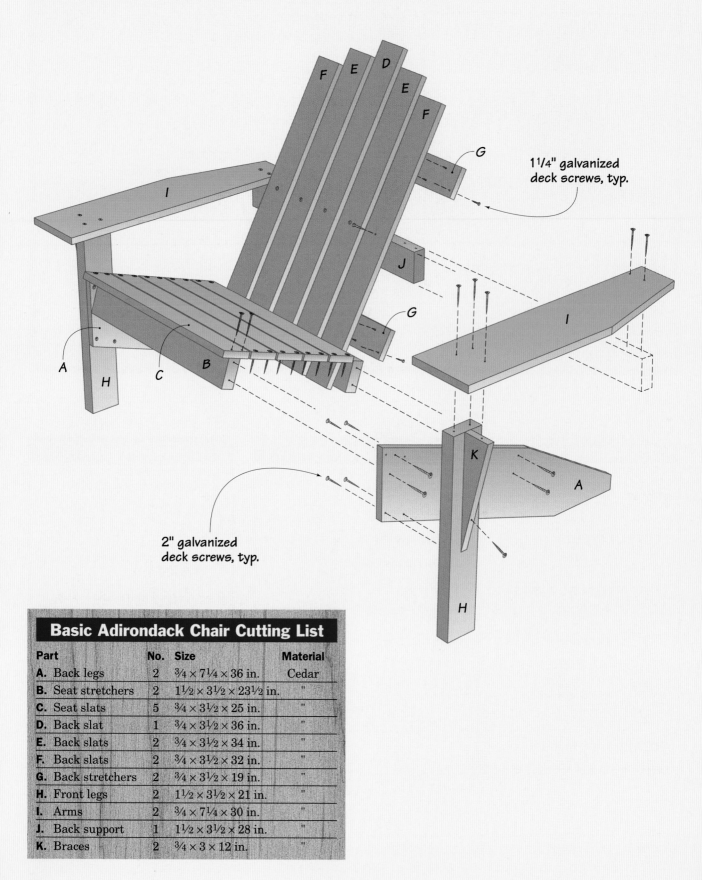

1¼" galvanized deck screws, typ.

2" galvanized deck screws, typ.

Basic Adirondack Chair Cutting List

Part	No.	Size	Material
A. Back legs	2	¾ × 7¼ × 36 in.	Cedar
B. Seat stretchers	2	1½ × 3½ × 23½ in.	"
C. Seat slats	5	¾ × 3½ × 25 in.	"
D. Back slat	1	¾ × 3½ × 36 in.	"
E. Back slats	2	¾ × 3½ × 34 in.	"
F. Back slats	2	¾ × 3½ × 32 in.	"
G. Back stretchers	2	¾ × 3½ × 19 in.	"
H. Front legs	2	1½ × 3½ × 21 in.	"
I. Arms	2	¾ × 7¼ × 30 in.	"
J. Back support	1	1½ × 3½ × 28 in.	"
K. Braces	2	¾ × 3 × 12 in.	"

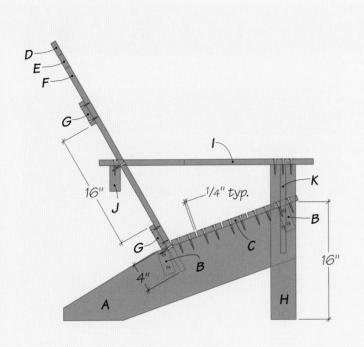

SIDE VIEW

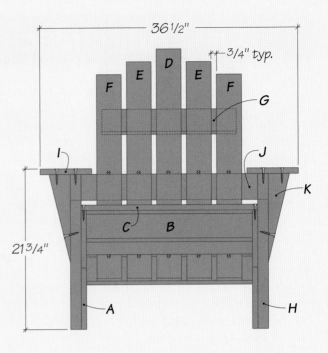

FRONT VIEW

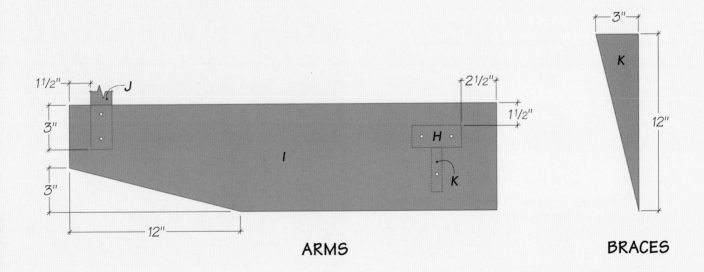

ARMS

BRACES

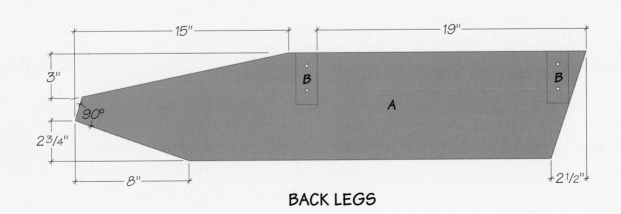

BACK LEGS

PHOTO A: Attach the back legs to the seat stretchers with 2-in. galvanized deck screws. Countersink the screw heads.

PHOTO B: Attach the back support, front legs and arm braces to the arm workpieces with 2-in. galvanized screws.

BUILD THE SEAT ASSEMBLY

❶ Cut the back legs to length from 1 × 8 stock. Follow the *Back Legs* drawing, page 11, to mark the angle cuts on the legs. Cut the leg angles with a jig saw or circular saw using a straightedge guide. Then cut the two seat stretchers to length.

❷ Attach the back legs to the seat stretchers. Position the face of the back stretcher 19 in. from the front ends of the legs and the leading edge of the front stretcher flush with the front ends of the legs. Mark the stretcher locations with a square, drill countersunk pilot holes through the legs and the stretchers, and fasten the parts with 2-in. galvanized deck screws **(See Photo A)**.

BUILD THE ARM ASSEMBLY

❸ Cut the front legs and the back support to length.

❹ Cut the arms and braces to size and shape. Mark for the angle cut on the back corner of each arm by measuring 12 in. along one long edge and 3 in. along the adjacent short end. Draw a line between these two points, and cut the angles with a jig saw guided by a straightedge. Save the triangular cutoff pieces; they'll become the arm braces.

❺ Measure and mark the positions of the front legs, braces, and back support on the arms (See *Arms* drawing, page 11). With the arms facedown on your workbench, use a combination square to mark the position of the front legs 2½ in. from the front of each arm and 1½ in. from the inside edges. Center and mark for a brace on the outside face of each leg. Then position the back support. It overlaps the inside edge of each arm by 3 in. and is inset 1½ in. from the ends.

❻ Build the arm assembly. Turn the arms faceup and drill countersunk pilot holes through the arms

for attaching the legs and back support. Attach the front legs and back support with 2-in. deck screws driven through the arms. Attach the braces to the arms and legs with countersunk 2-in. deck screws **(See Photo B)**.

ATTACH THE ARM & SEAT ASSEMBLIES

Fastening the arm and seat assemblies together will require the use of temporary braces and clamps. Cut two 21-in. lengths of scrap for the temporary braces.

❼ Stand up the arm assembly and set the temporary

PHOTO C: Install the seat. Clamp the seat assembly between the front legs. You'll need to set temporary braces beneath the arms to hold them level. Attach the seat assembly to the front legs with deck screws.

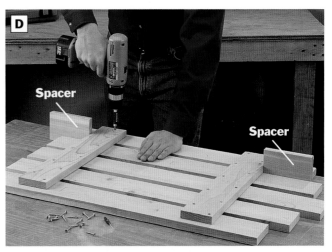

PHOTO D: Arrange the back slats facedown on the bench, and fasten the back stretchers to the slats with 1¼-in. galvanized deck screws. Insert ¾-in. scrap spacers between the slats to make alignment easy.

braces beneath the arms to hold the arm assembly level. Position the seat assembly between the front legs so the front ends of the back legs are flush with the front edges of the front legs. Clamp the two assemblies together. The top corner of the back legs should be 16 in. up from the bottom of the front legs.

❽ Fasten the seat assembly to the front legs with countersunk 2-in. deck screws. Drive the screws through the back legs into the front legs (**See Photo C**). Remove the temporary braces.

BUILD & ATTACH THE BACK

❾ Cut the back slats and the back stretchers to length. Assemble the back by laying the slats face-down on your workbench with the bottom edges flush. Position the stretchers so the lower stretcher is 4 in. from the bottom ends of the back slats, and there is 16 in. between the top and bottom stretchers. Drill countersunk pilot holes, and drive 1¼-in. deck screws through the stretchers into the slats (**See Photo D**).

❿ Install the chair back. Attach the chair back by sliding it into position with the lower back stretcher resting on the rear seat stretcher. Drill countersunk pilot holes through the back slats into the rear seat stretcher and the back support. Attach the back with 2-in. deck screws.

ATTACH THE SEAT SLATS

⓫ Cut the five seat slats to length, and attach them to the back legs with 2-in. deck screws. Countersink the screw holes, and use ¼-in. hardboard spacers to hold the slats evenly apart as you fasten the slats (**See Photo E**). NOTE: *You'll need to remove the chair*

arms one at a time to fasten the slats. Drive all the screws on one side of the seat, replace the arm, then remove the other arm and attach the slats.

FINISHING TOUCHES

⓬ Smooth all exposed chair surfaces and ease the corners with a sanding block. Apply the exterior sealer, stain or paint of your choice. Or leave the chair unfinished so it weathers naturally to gray.

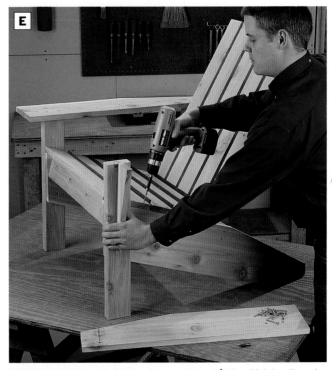

PHOTO E: Set the seat slats in place and insert ¼-in.-thick hardboard spacers between the slats. Remove one chair arm for drill clearance and fasten the seat slats to the back leg. Once the slats are attached on one side, reinstall the arm, remove the other arm and fasten the slats to the other back leg. Then reinstall the arm.

Advanced Adirondack Chair

This lively interpretation of the classic Adirondack chair emphasizes curves and comfort. Both the seat and the back are shaped to welcome you as you nestle in for a little reading or relaxation. Its high back slats have gently radiused ends, and the generously proportioned arms provide ample room for resting a snack or a cool drink. Building this piece of furniture takes a little time and skill, but the results are worth the effort.

Vital Statistics: Advanced Adirondack Chair

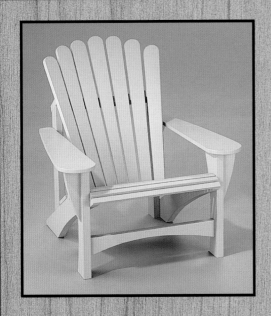

TYPE: Adirondack chair

OVERALL SIZE: $37\frac{1}{4}$W by $39\frac{1}{4}$L by $37\frac{3}{4}$H

MATERIAL: Pine

JOINERY: Butt joints reinforced with galvanized deck screws

CONSTRUCTION DETAILS:
· Chair parts are primed before assembly
· Seat and back assemblies are contoured
· Screws are countersunk, with the holes filled and sanded

FINISHING OPTIONS: Exterior latex primer and paint

Building time

 PREPARING STOCK
0 hours

 LAYOUT
3-4 hours

 CUTTING PARTS
4-6 hours

 ASSEMBLY
6-8 hours

 FINISHING
3-4 hours

TOTAL: 16-22 hours

Tools you'll use

· Circular saw
· Table saw (optional)
· Power miter saw (optional)
· Jig saw
· Compass (nail and string) or trammel points
· Drill/driver
· Clamps
· Combination square

Shopping list

☐ (2) 2 × 6 in. × 8 ft. pine
☐ (1) 2 × 4 in. × 6 ft. pine
☐ (1) 1 × 8 in. × 8 ft. pine
☐ (1) 1 × 6 in. × 6 ft. pine
☐ (5) 1 × 4 in. × 8 ft. pine
☐ Galvanized deck screws ($1\frac{1}{2}$-, 2-, $2\frac{1}{2}$-in.)
☐ Wood or auto body filler
☐ Latex primer
☐ Exterior latex paint

Advanced Adirondack Chair

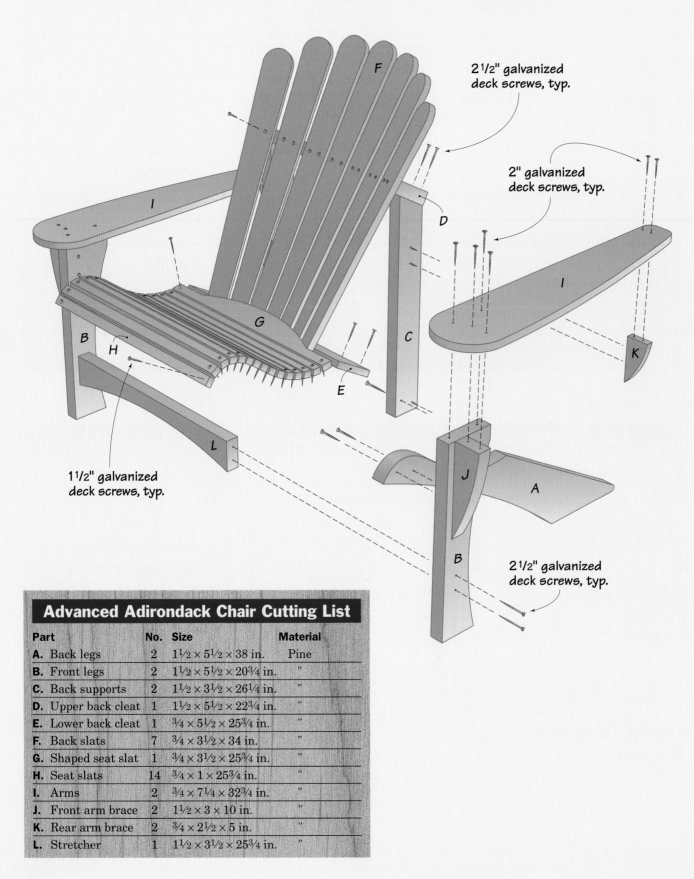

2 1/2" galvanized deck screws, typ.

2" galvanized deck screws, typ.

1 1/2" galvanized deck screws, typ.

2 1/2" galvanized deck screws, typ.

Advanced Adirondack Chair Cutting List

Part	No.	Size	Material
A. Back legs	2	$1^{1}/_{2} \times 5^{1}/_{2} \times 38$ in.	Pine
B. Front legs	2	$1^{1}/_{2} \times 5^{1}/_{2} \times 20^{3}/_{4}$ in.	"
C. Back supports	2	$1^{1}/_{2} \times 3^{1}/_{2} \times 26^{1}/_{4}$ in.	"
D. Upper back cleat	1	$1^{1}/_{2} \times 5^{1}/_{2} \times 22^{3}/_{4}$ in.	"
E. Lower back cleat	1	$^{3}/_{4} \times 5^{1}/_{2} \times 25^{3}/_{4}$ in.	"
F. Back slats	7	$^{3}/_{4} \times 3^{1}/_{2} \times 34$ in.	"
G. Shaped seat slat	1	$^{3}/_{4} \times 3^{1}/_{2} \times 25^{3}/_{4}$ in.	"
H. Seat slats	14	$^{3}/_{4} \times 1 \times 25^{3}/_{4}$ in.	"
I. Arms	2	$^{3}/_{4} \times 7^{1}/_{4} \times 32^{3}/_{4}$ in.	"
J. Front arm brace	2	$1^{1}/_{2} \times 3 \times 10$ in.	"
K. Rear arm brace	2	$^{3}/_{4} \times 2^{1}/_{2} \times 5$ in.	"
L. Stretcher	1	$1^{1}/_{2} \times 3^{1}/_{2} \times 25^{3}/_{4}$ in.	"

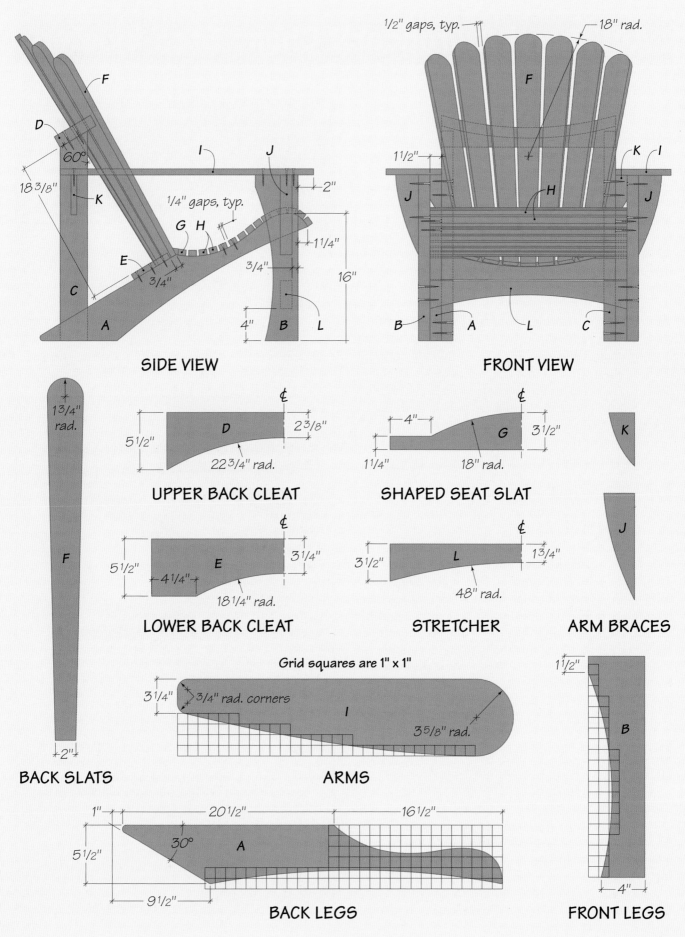

SIDE VIEW

FRONT VIEW

UPPER BACK CLEAT

SHAPED SEAT SLAT

LOWER BACK CLEAT

STRETCHER

ARM BRACES

BACK SLATS

Grid squares are 1" x 1"

ARMS

BACK LEGS

FRONT LEGS

PHOTO A: Make templates for the arms and legs, trace the parts onto blanks for the workpieces and cut the parts with a jig saw.

CUT OUT THE ARMS & LEGS

1 Cut pairs of blanks to length for the arms, front legs and back legs as specified on the *Cutting List,* page 16.

2 Refer to the drawings on page 17 to construct full-sized templates for the arms, front legs and back legs. Stiff cardboard will work if you plan to build only one of these chairs, but ¼-in. hardboard is a better choice because the template can be reused again and again. Bend a piece of flexible hardboard to help form the gradual curved profiles when you draw them on the templates. Cut the templates to shape, and smooth the edges as needed.

3 Lay the templates on the arm and leg workpieces, draw the shapes and cut out the arms and legs with a jig saw **(See Photo A)**.

MAKE THE BACK SLATS

The chair's back slats taper on both edges along their full length. You could shape the slats by first making a template from ¼-in. hardboard, tracing the profiles on the slat blanks, and then using a jig saw to cut out the slats. An alternate method is to build a simple clamping jig (See *Clamping Taper Jig,* right), to cut the tapered back slats on the table saw instead. The jig will allow you to make the tapered cuts quickly and produce smooth, flat edges on the slats.

4 Cut seven blanks for the back slats to length from 1 × 4 stock. NOTE: *All the slats start out the same length at this stage, but six of the seven will be trimmed to actual length later during chair assembly.*

5 Lay out the end radius and draw the tapered edges on the slat blanks, using the *Back Slats* drawing on page 17.

6 Cut the tapered edges on the back slats. If you use

Clamping taper jig

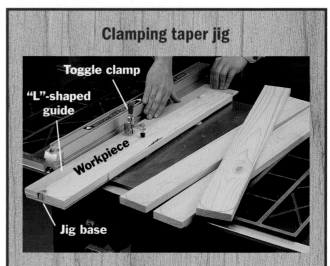

This clamping jig allows you to make tapered cuts on the table saw using the saw's rip fence as your guide. Build the jig by fastening a piece of ¾-in. "L"-shaped scrap to a length of ¼-in. plywood. The thin plywood serves as a base to support the workpieces, and the "L"-shaped piece guides the slats at an angle through the blade. Select the jig base from a piece of plywood longer than your back-slat workpieces. Cut the ¾-in. stock into an "L" shape, so the long inside edge of the "L" matches the taper angles you'll cut on the back slats. Fasten the jig parts so the back slats rest in the "L" guide, and one cutting line on the slat workpieces lines up with the edge of the jig base. Attach a toggle clamp to the jig to hold the workpieces in place as you cut. Slide the jig along the rip fence with the workpiece clamped in place to make the cuts. Once you cut the first taper, save the angled wastepiece—you'll need it to serve as a spacer for making the tapered cut along the opposite long edge of each slat.

the table saw and jig method for making these cuts, cut one tapered edge on each slat first. To do this, adjust the rip fence on the table saw so the jig rests against the rip fence, and the outside edge of the jig base is flush with the blade. Set the slats into the jig and clamp securely. Slide the jig and workpiece past the blade to make the first taper cuts.

7 Cut the second tapered edge on the back slats. Set one of the scrap wastepieces you made in Step 6 into the crook of the "L" on the jig, and flip each slat over in the jig so the tapered edge you just cut on the slats rests against the "L". This configuration should align the second taper cutting line on each workpiece with the edge of the jig base for making the second taper cuts. Clamp the slats in the jig and make the taper cuts **(See Photo B)**.

8 Cut the radiused ends of the slats with your jig saw. Sand the cuts smooth.

CUT THE REMAINING PROFILED PARTS
9 Cut the front and rear arm braces to size and shape. The exact curvature of the profiles on these parts isn't critical, but like parts should match.

10 Cut the upper back cleat, the lower back cleat, the shaped seat slat and the stretcher to size and shape. The profiles on these parts are simple arcs of various circles, and the radiuses are specified in the drawings on page 17. To establish the radiuses, first rip- and crosscut blanks for the parts. Clamp each workpiece to your benchtop. Find the centerline of the workpiece and extend the line onto the bench. Measure from the workpiece along the centerline the distance of the radius to establish the centerpoint for drawing the arc. Fashion a large compass by driving a nail into the worksurface at the centerpoint. Attach a string to the nail, and loop a pencil to the string at the appropriate radius. Mark arcs on the workpieces, and cut out the parts.

MAKE THE BACK SUPPORTS & SEAT SLATS
11 Crosscut the back supports to length, and trim the top ends to a 60° angle, as shown in the *Side View* drawing, page 17.

12 Cut the 14 seat slats to size. Rip ¾-in. stock to 1 in. wide on the table saw or with a circular saw. Cut the slats to length. Crosscutting the slats is quick to do with a power miter saw if you clamp a stop to the saw fence. Or you could also use a circular saw.

PHOTO B: Cut tapered edges on the back slats. We used a table saw jig for making these angled cuts. Once you've cut the first tapered edge, flip the slats over in the jig and cut the second tapered edge.

PHOTO C: Sand the chair parts smooth, and prime all surfaces with exterior latex primer. Primer will seal the wood and provide an even bonding surface for topcoating with paint.

PRIME THE PARTS
Because this chair is intended to remain outside in all kinds of weather and needs to be well sealed, it's a good idea to prime the surfaces of all the parts at this stage before you begin assembly. Also, since the chair will be assembled with screws but no glue, priming now will not affect glue bonds.

13 Sand and smooth all the chair parts. Prime the parts with latex-based primer **(See Photo C)**.

BUILD THE ARM ASSEMBLIES
14 Attach the front arm braces to the outside of the front legs, with the top edges flush. The braces should set back ¾ in. from the front edges of the front legs.

PHOTO D: Attach the arms to the arm braces on the front legs and back supports. Drive screws though the arms and down into the front legs as well. Drill countersunk pilot holes before you install the screws.

PHOTO E: Fasten the back legs to the inside face of the front legs and the outside face of the back supports with screws. Hold the parts in position with spring clamps to keep the parts from shifting.

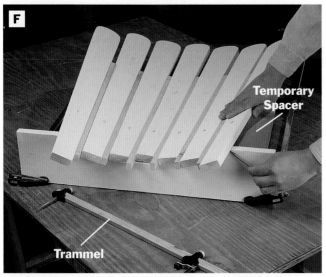

PHOTO F: Lay the back slats in place on the upper and lower back cleats. The tops of the back slats should follow the curve of an 18-in. radius. Mark the centerpoint of this radius on the center slat, and use a trammel or simple string compass to position the rest of the slats. Mark the slats for trimming where they intersect the lower back cleat.

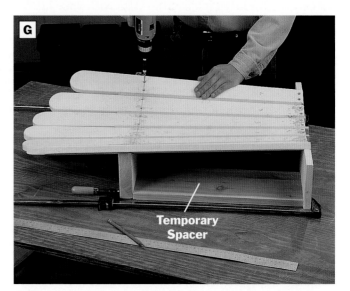

PHOTO G: Drill countersunk pilot holes for attaching the back slats to the upper and lower cleats. You may want to draw a reference line across the slats first to help establish screw placement on the upper back cleat. Attach the parts and remove the temporary spacer.

15 Attach the rear arm braces to the outside faces of the back supports, with the top edges of the braces set 20¾ in. from the bottom ends of the supports.

16 Attach the arms to the front legs and back supports with 2-in. galvanized deck screws **(See Photo D)**. Refer to the *Side View* and *Front View* drawings on page 17 for more information about exact placement of the arms.

17 Attach the back legs to the inner faces of the front legs and the outer faces of the back supports. Position the back legs so that the front tip of the back leg overhangs the front leg by 1¼ in. Adjust the parts until the measurement from the front edge of the front leg to the front edge of the back support is 27¼ in. Clamp the assemblies, drill countersunk pilot holes and attach the parts with 2½-in. galvanized deck screws **(See Photo E)**.

BUILD THE BACK ASSEMBLY

18 Cut two temporary spacers to hold the upper and lower back cleats in position while you attach the back slats. Cut the spacers 18⅜ in. long.

⓵ Stand the upper and lower back cleats on their flat back edges, and clamp the temporary spacers from Step 18 between the cleats. Lay the back slats into the curves on the cleats. Insert ½-in. spacers between the back slats to hold them evenly apart. Adjust the center back slat so it is even with the bottom face of the lower back cleat. Arrange the rest of the slats on the cleats so their top curved ends follow an 18-in.-radius arc. The easiest way to lay out this arc is to make a mark 18 in. from the top of the center slat and use this as the centerpoint for a trammel or string compass when you swing an arc. Adjust the back slats so the curved ends intersect with the end of the compass. Draw a line on the back slats where they cross the lower back cleat (**See Photo F**).

⓶ Remove the back slats and trim the bottom ends.

⓷ Reposition the slats on the back cleats, drill countersunk pilot holes and fasten the slats to the cleats with 2-in. galvanized deck screws (**See Photo G**).

ASSEMBLE THE CHAIR

⓸ Clamp the back assembly in position between the arm assemblies, with the lower back cleat held back ¾ in. from the point where the curved seat profile begins on the top edge of the back legs. The upper back cleat should rest on the back supports.

⓹ Install the stretcher between the front legs; this will keep the structure rigid while you attach the back assembly. Fasten the stretcher 4 in. up from the bottoms of the front legs.

⓺ Attach the back assembly. Fasten the lower cleat to the back legs with 2-in. galvanized deck screws and the upper back cleats into the back supports with 2½-in. deck screws (**See Photo H**).

⓻ Attach the seat slats. Remove the arms temporarily, for easier access to the screws. Attach the shaped seat slat first. Space the remaining seat slats evenly so they follow the full length of the curved profile on the back legs. Fasten the slats with countersunk 2-in. deck screws (**See Photo I**). Reattach the arms.

FINISHING TOUCHES

⓼ Fill all of the recessed screw holes with wood or auto body filler. Let the filler dry and sand smooth. Spot-prime the filled screw heads.

⓽ Brush on two coats of exterior latex paint.

PHOTO H: Set the back assembly in place between the two arm assemblies and clamp the parts together. Drive screws through the upper and lower cleats into the back supports and back legs.

PHOTO I: Remove the arm pieces to provide clearance for attaching the seat slats. Install the seat slats along the profiled areas of the back legs starting with the shaped seat slat. Space the slats evenly apart along the back leg. A ¼-in.-thick scrap spacer will help keep the slat spacing uniform as you install the slats.

Patio Table & Chairs

This patio table and chair set is significantly more formal than the traditional picnic table and benches, yet it is very easy to build. Made entirely of cedar for all-weather durability and beauty, this table will be the centerpiece of many memorable summer meals for you and your family. And if you need a table that is slightly larger, it's a simple matter to expand the table length and build a couple more chairs.

Vital Statistics: Patio Table & Chairs

TYPE: Patio table and chairs

OVERALL SIZE: Table: 48W by 48L by 30H
Chairs: 18W by 23L by 36½H

MATERIAL: Cedar

JOINERY: Butt joints reinforced with galvanized deck screws

CONSTRUCTION DETAILS:
- Many parts on both the table and chairs are chamfered to minimize sharp edges
- Table aprons reinforced with corner braces to strengthen leg joints

FINISHING OPTIONS: Penetrating UV protectant sealer or leave unfinished to weather naturally to gray

Building time

PREPARING STOCK
0 hours

LAYOUT
3-4 hours

CUTTING PARTS
2-3 hours

ASSEMBLY
6-8 hours

FINISHING
2-4 hours

TOTAL: 13-19 hours

Tools you'll use

- Table saw
- Power miter saw
- Router table and piloted chamfering bit
- Drill/driver
- Clamps
- Combination square

Shopping list

- ☐ (2) 4 × 4 in. × 6 ft. or (1) 4 × 4 in. × 10 ft. cedar
- ☐ (3) 2 × 8 in. × 10 ft. cedar
- ☐ (5) 2 × 6 in. × 8 ft. cedar
- ☐ (4) 2 × 4 in. × 8 ft. cedar
- ☐ (9) 1 × 4 in. × 8 ft. cedar
- ☐ (4) 1 × 2 in. × 6 ft. cedar
- ☐ Galvanized deck screws (2-, 2½-in.)
- ☐ Finishing materials

Patio Table & Chairs

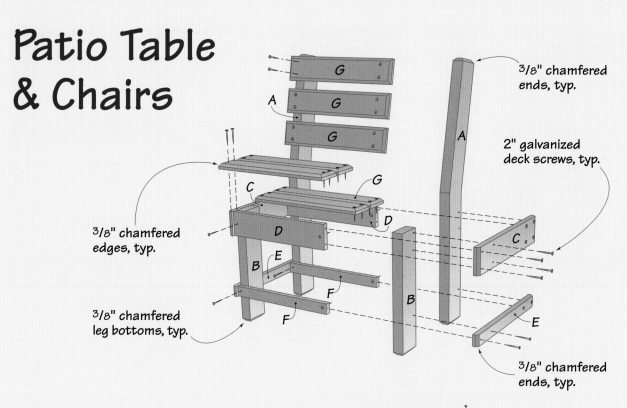

3/8" chamfered ends, typ.

2" galvanized deck screws, typ.

3/8" chamfered edges, typ.

3/8" chamfered leg bottoms, typ.

3/8" chamfered ends, typ.

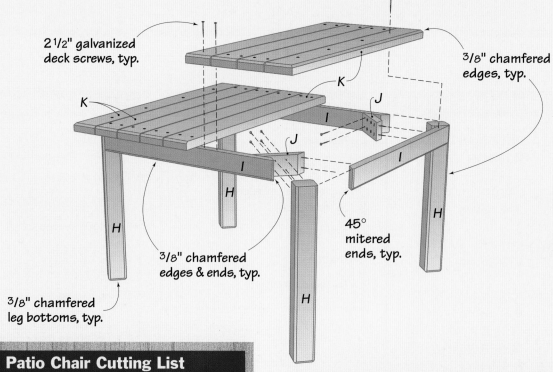

2 1/2" galvanized deck screws, typ.

3/8" chamfered edges, typ.

45° mitered ends, typ.

3/8" chamfered edges & ends, typ.

3/8" chamfered leg bottoms, typ.

Patio Chair Cutting List

Part	No.	Size	Material
A. Back legs	2	$1\frac{1}{2} \times 7\frac{1}{4} \times 36\frac{1}{2}$ in.	Cedar
B. Front legs	2	$1\frac{1}{2} \times 3\frac{1}{2} \times 16\frac{1}{2}$ in.	"
C. Upper frame sides	2	$\frac{3}{4} \times 3\frac{1}{2} \times 17\frac{1}{2}$ in.	"
D. Upper frame ends	2	$\frac{3}{4} \times 3\frac{1}{2} \times 16$ in.	"
E. Lower frame sides	2	$\frac{3}{4} \times 1\frac{1}{2} \times 17\frac{1}{2}$ in.	"
F. Lower frame ends	2	$\frac{3}{4} \times 1\frac{1}{2} \times 16$ in.	"
G. Slats	7	$\frac{3}{4} \times 3\frac{1}{2} \times 18$ in.	"

Patio Table Cutting List

Part	No.	Size	Material
H. Legs	4	$3\frac{1}{2} \times 3\frac{1}{2} \times 28\frac{1}{2}$ in.	Cedar
I. Aprons	4	$1\frac{1}{2} \times 3\frac{1}{2} \times 38$ in.	"
J. Braces	4	$1\frac{1}{2} \times 3\frac{1}{2} \times 9\frac{1}{8}$ in.	"
K. Top slats	9	$1\frac{1}{2} \times 5\frac{1}{8} \times 48$ in.	"

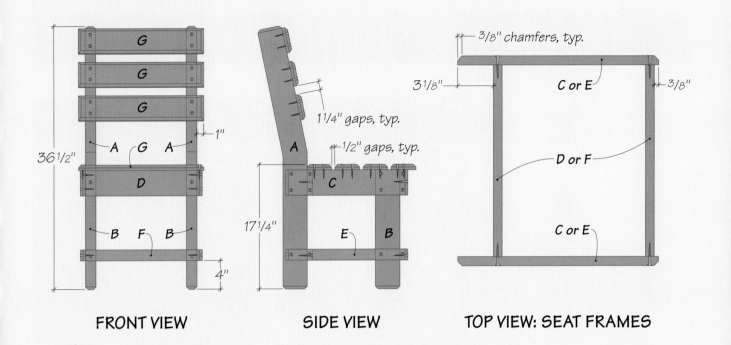

FRONT VIEW

SIDE VIEW

TOP VIEW: SEAT FRAMES

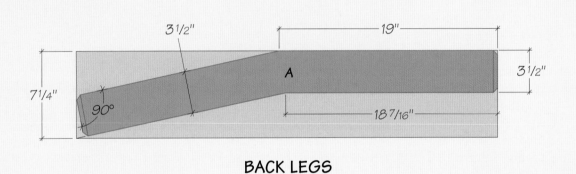

BACK LEGS

FRONT VIEW

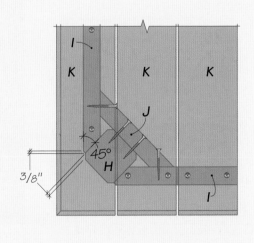

TOP VIEW: CORNER DETAIL

BUILD THE CHAIRS

Since you're building four identical chairs, cut parts for all the chairs and build them simultaneously. In this situation, make sure your measurements are accurate before cutting all the pieces.

❶ Make the back legs. Cut blanks to length from 2 × 8 stock, and lay out the legs **(See Photo A)** following the measurements in the *Back Legs* drawing, page 25. Cut out the back legs with a jig saw. After cutting the legs to shape, chamfer the top and bottom ends of the legs, using a router table with a piloted chamfering bit set to ³⁄₈ in.

PHOTO A: Lay out and cut eight back chair legs to shape. Use the *Back Legs* drawing, page 25, to establish reference points for drawing the leg shapes. Connect the points with a straightedge.

❷ Build the upper and lower seat frames. The construction of both frames is identical, but the width of the parts is different. Cut the upper and lower side and end pieces to size for both frames. Rout ³⁄₈-in. chamfers along the outside ends of the side pieces. Clamp each frame together using the *Top View: Seat Frames* drawing, page 25, as a guide for positioning the parts. Drill countersunk pilot holes through the sides, and fasten the frames together with 2-in. galvanized deck screws **(See Photo B)**.

❸ Make the front legs. Cut the legs to length from 2 × 4 stock, and chamfer all four edges of the bottom ends of each leg.

PHOTO B: Build an upper and lower frame for each chair. Note that the end pieces of each frame are inset ³⁄₈ in. and 3¹⁄₈ in. from the ends of the side pieces. Clamp the frame parts together, and drive 2-in. galvanized deck screws through the sides and into the ends to make the frames.

4 Screw the legs and frames together. Attach the frames to the back legs first, with the top edge of the upper frame 16½ in. above the leg bottom. Place the bottom frame 4 in. from the leg bottom. Then clamp the front legs in position inside the front corners of both frames, and fasten with galvanized deck screws (**See Photo C**).

5 Make the slats. All the slats are the same length and shape, but the position of the attachment screws is different between the back slats and the seat slats. Cut the slats to length from 1 × 4 stock, and chamfer all four edges of one side. Designate 12 slats (three per chair) as back slats, and mark centerlines for the attachment screws. These back slats will attach to the back legs. Next, measure and mark centerlines for the attachment screws in the seat slats. These slats fasten to the upper frame sides. Drill countersunk pilot holes along the lines in all the slats, two screws per joint.

6 Attach the slats. Align the top edge of the uppermost back slat as shown in the *Front* and *Side View* drawings, page 25, and leave 1¼-in. spaces between the slats. Leave ½-in. spaces between the seat slats, with the rear seat slat held tight against the back legs. Fasten the slats with countersunk galvanized deck screws (**See Photo D**).

BUILD THE TABLE

All visible corners and ends of the table legs, aprons and slats are chamfered. Although you can use a handheld router and a piloted chamfering bit, a router table makes the task quicker and easier. Chamfers for all parts are cut at the same ⅜-in. height setting.

PHOTO C: Attach the upper and lower frames to the back and front legs with countersunk screws.

PHOTO D: To create uniform slat spacing, use a ½-in. spacer for positioning the seat slats and a 1¼-in. spacer for the back slats. Start the back slats at the bottom of the back leg angle. Install the seat slats so the back seat slat butts against the back legs.

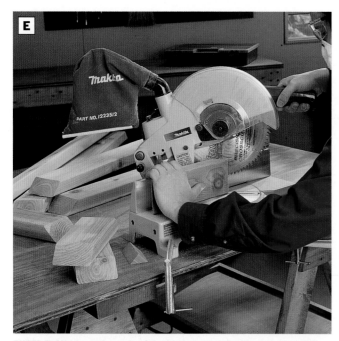

PHOTO E: Miter-cut the ends of the leg braces and table aprons to 45°. The safest way to make these cuts, particularly on the short leg braces, is to use a power miter saw or table saw rather than a circular saw.

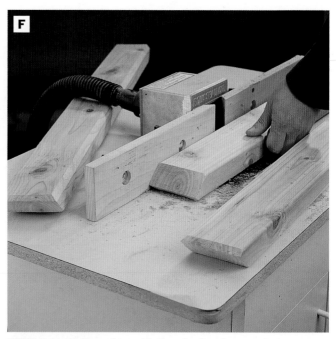

PHOTO F: The bottom edge and both ends of each apron piece are chamfered. Make these cuts at the router table, using a piloted chamfering bit set to a height of 3/8 in.

PHOTO G: Assemble the table legs, aprons and corner braces. Attach the parts by driving 2½-in. galvanized deck screws through countersunk pilot holes in the leg braces. Fasten the brace to each apron with a pair of screws driven in at an angle into the aprons, and use four screws for securing the leg. Be sure the legs are tight against the aprons and braces as you drive the screws.

❼ Make the legs. Cut the legs to length from 4 × 4 stock. Chamfer all four long edges and the edges of the leg bottoms.

❽ Make the aprons and braces. Cut the aprons and braces to length, and miter-cut the ends at 45° **(See Photo E)**. When mitering these parts, use extra care to cut accurately.

❾ Chamfer one edge and both ends on one face of each apron **(See Photo F)**. Since the apron ends are mitered, there is less surface to guide against the router table fence when chamfering. One solution is to clamp the aprons together with the ends flush and rout all the ends in one pass. NOTE: *If you are using a handheld router, the mitered ends don't provide a surface for the chamfer bit bearing to guide against. Clamp the aprons together on your worksurface, with the ends flush. Position and clamp a straightedge across the aprons to use as a guide for the router base before making the cuts.*

10 Assemble the table legs, aprons and braces. First drill six countersunk pilot holes in the braces—four holes for attaching the leg and two holes angled at each end for the aprons, as shown in the *Top View: Corner Detail* drawing, page 25. Stand the legs upside down on the floor or your worksurface, position the aprons and braces around each leg, and attach the parts with galvanized deck screws (**See Photo G**).

11 Make the nine top slats. Cut the slats to length, and rip them to width on the table saw (**See Photo H**). Chamfer the outer edge of the two end slats on your router table. Chamfer the top edges of the ends of the slats.

12 Drill pilot holes in the slats. Lay a slat across the table structure, with an equal overhang on both ends. Mark the centerpoint of the aprons on the edge of the slat and transfer these marks to the face of the slat. Use this first slat as a guide to mark screw locations on all the slats. Drill countersunk pilot holes along the guidelines on all the slats, two holes per joint.

13 Attach the slats. Determine the centerline of the table and install the center slat over this line. Use two 3/16-in.-thick spacers to establish the slat gaps. Install slats out from the center slat, fastening each with galvanized deck screws (**See Photo I**).

FINISHING TOUCHES
14 Sand the table and chairs well to smooth the surfaces and edges. Make sure all screws are countersunk below the surface of the wood.

15 Apply a clear UV protectant sealer or leave unfinished to weather naturally to gray.

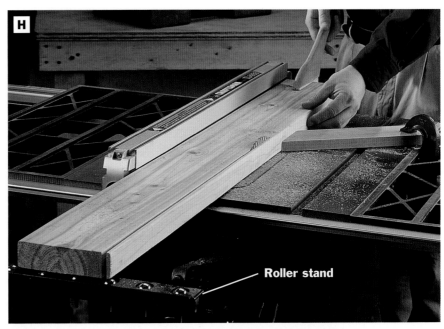

Roller stand

PHOTO H: Rip-cut 2 × 6 stock down to a width of 5 1/8 in. to form the tabletop slats. You could make these cuts with a circular saw and straightedge guide, but a better choice is to use the table saw and rip fence. Support workpieces with a roller stand as they leave the saw table.

PHOTO I: Attach the top slats to the aprons with 2 1/2-in. deck screws. Fasten the center slat first, then work outward. This way, the overhang will be consistent on both ends of the table, and the slats will be evenly positioned. Use a pair of 3/16-in. spacers to create uniform gaps between the slats.

Tiletop BBQ Center

Can't you just smell the charcoal already? Outdoor cooking is often the centerpiece of summer gatherings, and when you get together with family and friends for barbecued ribs, grilled steaks or juicy burgers, this attractive outdoor grilling accessory will make the chef's job so efficient that he or she will be able to enjoy the conversation as well. Then, if the conversation lags, you can casually let people know that you built this versatile cart yourself, in just a weekend's worth of time. Impression guaranteed.

Vital Statistics: Tiletop BBQ Center

TYPE: Tiletop BBQ center

OVERALL SIZE: $26\frac{7}{8}$W by $44\frac{1}{4}$L by $35\frac{1}{2}$H

MATERIAL: Cedar, ceramic tile

JOINERY: Butt joints reinforced with galvanized screws

CONSTRUCTION DETAILS:
- Ceramic tiles laid on exterior plywood subbase
- Integral handle and wheels for easy moving
- Recessed condiment shelf

FINISHING OPTIONS: Penetrating UV protectant sealer, exterior paint or leave unfinished and allow to weather naturally to gray

---

Building time

PREPARING STOCK
0 hours

LAYOUT
1-2 hours

CUTTING PARTS
2-3 hours

ASSEMBLY
5-6 hours

FINISHING
2-3 hours

TOTAL: 10-14 hours

Tools you'll use

- Circular saw
- Power miter saw
- Compass
- Jig saw
- Drill/driver
- Clamps
- Hammer, nailset
- Combination square
- Tiling tools ($\frac{1}{4}$-in. notched trowel, grout float, sponge)
- Hacksaw

Shopping list

- ☐ (1) $\frac{3}{4}$ in. × 4 × 4 ft. exterior plywood
- ☐ (1) $\frac{3}{4}$ in.-dia. × 24-in. hardwood dowel
- ☐ (2) 2 × 6 in. × 8 ft. cedar
- ☐ (1) 2 × 4 in. × 6 ft. cedar
- ☐ (2) 1 × 6 in. × 8 ft. cedar
- ☐ (2) 1 × 6 in. × 6 ft. cedar
- ☐ Galvanized deck screws (2-, 3-in.)
- ☐ 6d galvanized finish nails
- ☐ (48) $4\frac{1}{4}$ × $4\frac{1}{4}$-in. glazed ceramic tiles
- ☐ Thinset mortar, tile grout
- ☐ (2) 6-in.-dia. wheels; $\frac{1}{2}$-in.-dia. × 24-in. steel rod, washers, cotter pins
- ☐ UV protectant sealer

31

Tiletop BBQ Center

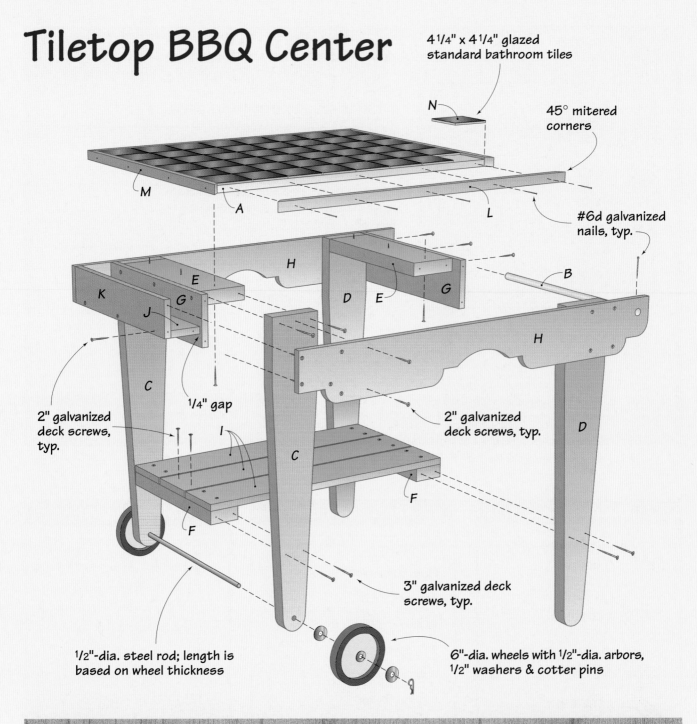

4¼" x 4¼" glazed standard bathroom tiles

N

45° mitered corners

#6d galvanized nails, typ.

M

A

L

H

E

K

J

G

D

E

G

B

C

¼" gap

2" galvanized deck screws, typ.

I

C

2" galvanized deck screws, typ.

F

H

D

F

3" galvanized deck screws, typ.

½"-dia. steel rod; length is based on wheel thickness

6"-dia. wheels with ½"-dia. arbors, ½" washers & cotter pins

Tiletop BBQ Center Cutting List							
Part	**No.**	**Size**	**Material**	**Part**	**No.**	**Size**	**Material**
A. Plywood subtop	1	$\frac{3}{4} \times 26\frac{1}{8} \times 34\frac{7}{8}$ in.	Exterior plywood	**G.** End aprons	2	$\frac{3}{4} \times 5\frac{1}{2} \times 20$ in.	Cedar
B. Handle	1	$\frac{3}{4}$ dia. $\times 21\frac{1}{2}$ in.	Hardwood dowel	**H.** Side aprons	2	$\frac{3}{4} \times 5\frac{1}{2} \times 44\frac{1}{4}$ in.	"
C. Front legs	2	$1\frac{1}{2} \times 5\frac{1}{2} \times 32\frac{7}{8}$ in.	Cedar	**I.** Shelf slats	3	$\frac{3}{4} \times 5\frac{1}{2} \times 31\frac{3}{4}$ in.	"
D. Back legs	2	$1\frac{1}{2} \times 5\frac{1}{2} \times 34\frac{1}{2}$ in.	"	**J.** Condiment shelf	1	$\frac{3}{4} \times 3\frac{1}{2} \times 20$ in.	"
E. Upper crosspieces	2	$1\frac{1}{2} \times 5\frac{1}{2} \times 17$ in.	"	**K.** Condiment front	1	$\frac{3}{4} \times 4 \times 20$ in.	"
F. Lower crosspieces	2	$1\frac{1}{2} \times 3\frac{1}{2} \times 17$ in.	"	**L.** Top side edging	2	$\frac{3}{4} \times 1 \times 36\frac{3}{8}$ in.	"
				M. Top end edging	2	$\frac{3}{4} \times 1 \times 27\frac{5}{8}$ in.	"
				N. Tiles	48	$\frac{1}{4} \times 4\frac{1}{4} \times 4\frac{1}{4}$ in.	Glazed bathroom tile

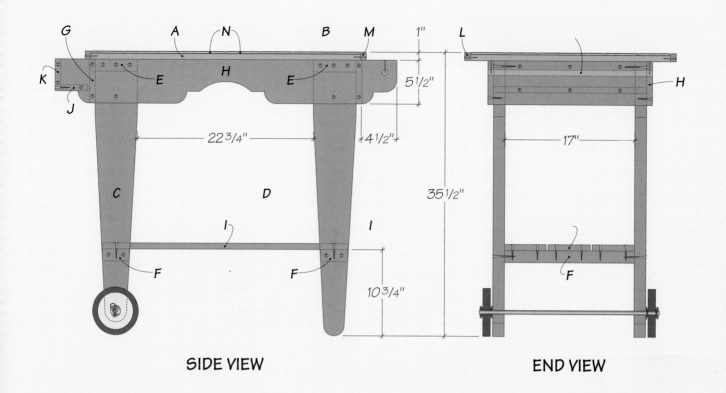

SIDE VIEW

END VIEW

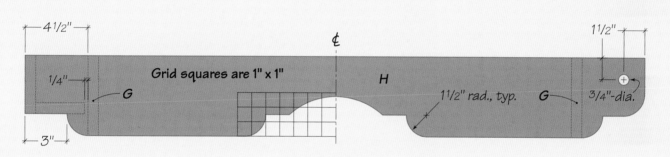

SIDE APRONS

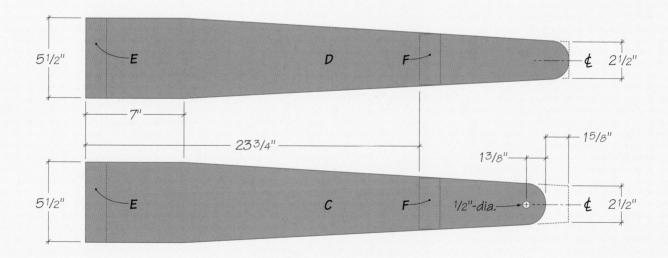

FRONT & BACK LEGS

PHOTO A: Once you've cut the leg tapers and shortened the front legs, mark and cut the rounded feet with a jig saw. Clamp each leg to your workbench to make sawing the feet easier.

BUILD THE LEG ASSEMBLIES

1 Crosscut the legs to size. Cut identical blanks for all four legs, even though the front legs will eventually be shortened to allow clearance for the wheels.

2 Measure and mark the location of the lower crosspieces on the inside faces of the legs. Position the upper face of the crosspieces 10¾ in. from the bottom of the legs. Extend the marks across the legs with a combination square.

3 Cut identical tapers on all four legs (See *Front & Back Legs* drawings, page 33). The tapers begin 7 in. from the tops of the legs and reduce them to 2½ in. at the bottom. Draw the foot radius on the two back legs with a compass.

4 Cut 1⅝ in. off the bottom ends of the front legs, then mark for the 1⅜-in. foot radius. When you draw the foot radii, the pivot point for the compass marks the center-point of the wheel axle.

5 Clamp each leg to your work-surface and cut the curved foot profiles on all four legs with a jig saw (**See Photo A**).

6 Bore the ½-in.-dia. axle hole in the front legs. You may want to mount your drill in a right-angle drilling guide to ensure that these axle holes are straight.

PHOTO B: Fasten the legs to the upper and lower crosspieces with deck screws. Position the upper faces of the lower crosspieces so they are 10¾ in. from the bottoms of the legs.

7 Cut the upper and lower cross-pieces to length. Set the cross-pieces between the legs, and hold the parts in place with clamps. Drill countersunk pilot holes through the legs into the cross-pieces, and attach the legs to the crosspieces with 3-in. galvanized deck screws (**See Photo B**).

CUT THE REMAINING PARTS

Cedar is commonly sold smooth on one side and rough on the other. For the 1× apron, slat and condiment parts, you could choose to have the rough side facing out or in, depending upon the surface appearance you prefer. Building the cart with workpieces facing smooth-side-out will lead to fewer splinters later and will be easier to keep clean.

8 Make the side aprons. Cut the two apron blanks to length. Transfer the side apron profile (See *Side Aprons* drawing, page 33) to one of the blanks, and mark the centerpoint of the handle dowel hole. Stack the marked blank on top of the unmarked one with the edges aligned, and clamp the blanks together on your worksurface. Gang-cut the profile on both aprons at once with your jig saw. Sand the cut edges smooth.

9 Bore the ¾-in.-dia. handle dowel holes while the side aprons are still clamped together.

10 Cut the end aprons, shelf slats and handle dowel to length.

11 Cut the condiment shelf and front to size. First rip 1 × 6 stock to width (See *Cutting List*, page 32), then cut the pieces to length.

PHOTO C: Attach the end aprons to the legs, then turn the leg assemblies upside down and fasten the side aprons in place. Hold the parts in position with clamps while you drive the screws.

PHOTO D: Fasten the shelf slats in position, then attach the condiment shelf and front to the side aprons. Leave a ¼-in. gap between the condiment shelf and the end apron (See *Side Aprons* drawing, page 33), to allow for water drainage. Use 2-in. galvanized deck screws on these parts.

PHOTO E: Arrange rows of tiles to determine the length and width of the tile top. NOTE: *You may need to space the tiles to allow for grout lines if your tiles don't have self-spacing nubs on the edges.* The overall dimensions will establish the size of the plywood subtop.

PHOTO F: Spread a layer of thinset mortar over the subtop using a ¼-in. notched trowel. Press the tiles into the mortar in a systematic fashion, working out from one corner both lengthwise and widthwise. Keep watch on your tile spacing to ensure that all the tiles will fit on the subtop.

ASSEMBLE THE WORKSTATION

⓬ Attach the end aprons to the leg assemblies with 2-in. galvanized deck screws. Fasten the parts by screwing through the end aprons and into the upper crosspieces and legs. NOTE: *Make sure that the longer back legs are at the same end of the aprons as the handle dowel holes.*

⓭ Fasten the side aprons to the leg assemblies. Stand leg assemblies upside down on your work surface with the end aprons facing out. Clamp the side aprons in place so they extend 4½ in. beyond the the end aprons on both ends of the cart. Drill countersunk pilot holes, and attach the side aprons to the leg assemblies with 2-in. screws, four screws per joint **(See Photo C)**.

⓮ Install the shelf slats. Stand the workstation right-side-up on the floor. Put a 1½-in.-thick board under the shorter front legs to hold the workstation approximately level. Position the shelf slats so their ends are flush with the outer edges of the lower crossbraces and there are equal gaps between the slats. Drill countersunk pilot holes through the slats and into the lower crosspieces, and fasten the slats in place.

⓯ Attach the condiment shelf and front pieces. Start by drilling countersunk pilot holes in the side aprons on the end opposite the cart handle. Position the shelf ¾ in. from the ends of the side aprons to allow space for attaching the condiment front. Make sure there is about a ¼-in. gap between the shelf and the end apron to allow for water drainage. Fasten the shelf between the side aprons with 2-in. screws. Install the front by attaching it to the side aprons and the shelf with 2-in. screws (**See Photo D**).

BUILD THE TOP

The sizes of the plywood top and edging are based on the assumption that the tiles are 4¼ in. square and grout lines between the tiles are all ⅛ in. We did not leave a distinct grout line between the tile and the edging because this is an outdoor project, and the wood edging will expand and contract with changes in humidity. If you use a different size tile, you will need to modify the overall size of the top. Be sure to also factor in the space needed for grout lines.

🔟 Determine the plywood top size by laying out lines of tiles to mark the length and width of the workstation top (**See Photo E**). Cut the plywood subtop to size, taking care that it is square.

🔟 Fasten the top to the workstation. Position the subtop so there is an even overhang all around, and attach it with 2-in. screws driven through the upper crosspieces from below (attaching the top from below allows you the option of removing the top later on without destroying the tile).

🔟 Apply an even layer of thinset mortar to the subtop with a ¼-in. notched trowel. Be sure to wear gloves when working with mortar or grout.

🔟 Set the tiles into the mortar (**See Photo F**). If you are not an experienced tile setter and your tiles are not self-spacing, we recommend starting at one corner of the top and setting one line of tile across the width and one line across the length. This allows you to verify the exact size of the grout lines, since it will be easier to

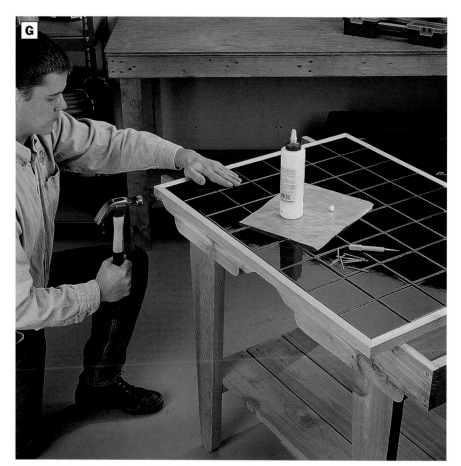

PHOTO G: Wrap the tile top with ¾ × 1-in. cedar edging, mitering the corners. Fasten the edging pieces with wood glue and 6d galvanized finish nails, nailing into the plywood subtop. Then recess the nailheads with a nailset.

adjust the positioning of these first few guide tiles, if need be, than to reposition the whole top-full of tiles. Press the tiles firmly into the thinset mortar to ensure that they seat fully and will not come loose. Allow the mortar to dry thoroughly before continuing to finish the top.

🔟 Make and install the edging. Rip ¾ × 1-in. strips from 1 × 6 stock, and crosscut the edging to length. Miter-cut the ends to 45°. Drill pilot holes, and attach the edging to the edges of the subtop with glue and #6d galvanized finish nails (**See Photo G**). Recess the nailheads with a nailset.

🔟 Apply the grout. Select a grout color that complements your tile; generally speaking, darker grout

shows spotting and stains much less than lighter-colored grout. Mix powdered grout according to the manufacturer's instructions to produce a relatively dry mixture that retains its shape when you ball it in your hand. Protect the top surface of the wood edging with masking tape.

🔟 Spread grout across the tiles and into the joints, using a grout float (**See Photo H**). Work diagonally across the tabletop to avoid digging the grout out of some joints as you fill others.

🔟 Wipe away the excess grout. Again working with diagonal strokes, use a sponge to remove the excess grout from the tile surface (**See Photo I**). Rinse the sponge frequently and get the top

PHOTO H: Press grout into the gaps between the tiles using a grout float. Work diagonally across the surface, pulling the float toward you as you go. Working diagonally helps to minimize the chances of accidentally pulling grout out of the gaps you've already filled.

PHOTO I: Remove excess grout and smooth the grout lines with a water-dampened sponge. Again, work diagonally. Continue wiping the tiles, rinsing the sponge and wringing it out until the tiles are clean. Wipe away haze left by the grout with a soft cloth.

clean before the grout has a chance to fully set. As the grout dries, any grout residue will appear as a hazy film on the tiles. Wipe them clean with a soft, dry cloth.

INSTALL THE WHEELS

㉔ Cut the 1/2-in.-dia. axle rod to length with a hacksaw. To accommodate the washers and cotter pins, the axles must extend beyond the legs 3/4 in. plus the thickness of the wheel hub on each side. Wheel hub dimensions will vary. Thus, if your wheel hubs are 1 in. thick, the axles need to be at least 23 1/2 in. long.

㉕ Drill holes in the axle for the cotter pins. To do this easily, make a wooden cradle by cutting a V-shaped groove into the face of an 8- to 12-in. piece of 2 × 4 with two passes of your saw set at a 45° angle. Fasten the grooved 2 × 4 to a slightly larger piece of 3/4-in. scrap.

Clamp the cradle to your drill press table to support the axle while you drill it. Set the axle in the groove and drill a ⅛-in. hole through the axle near (verify the exact position) each end of the rod (**See Photo J**). TIP: *Use a slow speed setting on the drill press and lubricate the bit with a drop of light machine oil to keep the bit from overheating.*

❷❻ Install the wheels. Slide the axle into place on the legs, slip washers onto the axle next to the legs to serve as spacers, slide the wheels and another set of washers onto the axle, and insert the cotter pins to lock the wheels in place (**See Photo K**).

FINISHING TOUCHES

❷❼ Check that all nailheads are set and all screw heads are countersunk slightly below the surface of the wood. You can either fill nail- and screw head recesses with wood putty or simply leave the heads exposed for a more rustic appearance.

❷❽ Sand all exposed surfaces and edges, then apply the finish of your choice. We used a clear penetrating exterior wood sealer with good UV protection in order to retain and highlight the natural beauty of the wood. Depending on the tile you've selected for your top, you could elect to paint the workstation for a more dramatic look. Or, as with any cedar furniture, you may leave it unfinished and let it weather to a silvery gray.

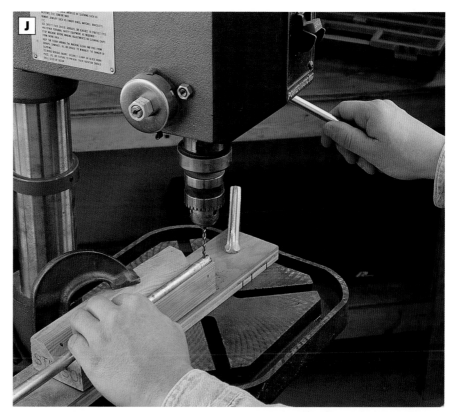

PHOTO J: Cut a V-shaped notch in a scrap of 2 × 4 to help steady the axle as you drill holes for cotter pins. Fasten the notched cradle to another scrap, and clamp the jig to the drill press table. Drill through the rod using a slow speed setting and firm—but not excessive—force on the bit.

PHOTO K: Insert the axle through the holes in the front legs, then install washers, wheels and cotter pins to secure the wheels. The washers next to the cotter pins keep the wheels from rubbing against the cotter pins as the wheels turn.

Frame-style Sandbox

Turn off your TV and put away those video games. Instead, get out the old spatulas and pans and cars and trucks. Here's a simple project to build that will give your children or grand-children hours of fun. And, if you're lucky, they'll even let you play with them. Built completely from 2 × 4s, this project can easily be completed—even with little helpers—in a weekend. If you elect to use cedar rather than treated lumber and not paint it, the sandbox can easily be completed in an afternoon. Got a big family? Simply lengthen the side boards to make the sand-box whatever size works best for you.

Vital Statistics: Frame-style Sandbox

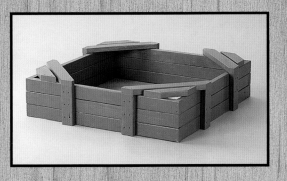

TYPE: Sandbox

OVERALL SIZE: 51W by 51L by 12H

MATERIAL: Treated lumber

JOINERY: Butt joints reinforced with galvanized deck screws

CONSTRUCTION DETAILS:
- Design is easily expandable
- Corner braces double as children's benches
- Corner joints alternate from tier to tier for strength
- Straightforward joinery speeds construction

FINISHING OPTIONS: Exterior latex primer and paint

Building time

PREPARING STOCK
0 hours

LAYOUT
1-2 hours

CUTTING PARTS
1-2 hours

ASSEMBLY
1-2 hours

FINISHING
2-4 hours

TOTAL: 5-10 hours

Tools you'll use

- Power miter saw or circular saw
- Drill/driver
- Combination square

Shopping list

- ☐ (9) 2 × 4 in. × 8 ft. treated lumber
- ☐ Galvanized deck screws (2½-, 3-in.)
- ☐ Latex primer
- ☐ Exterior latex paint

Frame-style Sandbox

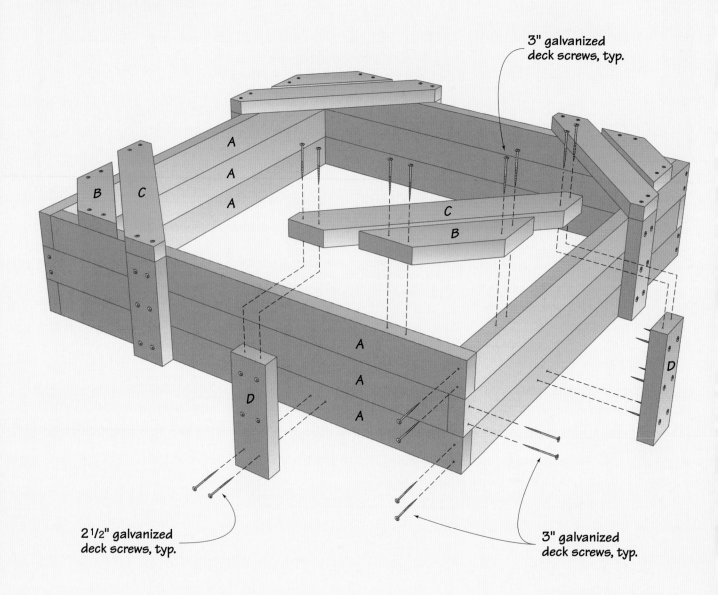

3" galvanized deck screws, typ.

2 1/2" galvanized deck screws, typ.

3" galvanized deck screws, typ.

Sandbox Cutting List			
Part	No.	Size	Material
A. Side tiers	12	$1\frac{1}{2} \times 3\frac{1}{2} \times 46\frac{1}{2}$ in.	Treated lumber
B. Short seats	4	$1\frac{1}{2} \times 3\frac{1}{2} \times 14\frac{1}{2}$ in.	"
C. Long seats	4	$1\frac{1}{2} \times 3\frac{1}{2} \times 25$ in.	"
D. Braces	8	$1\frac{1}{2} \times 3\frac{1}{2} \times 10\frac{1}{2}$ in.	"

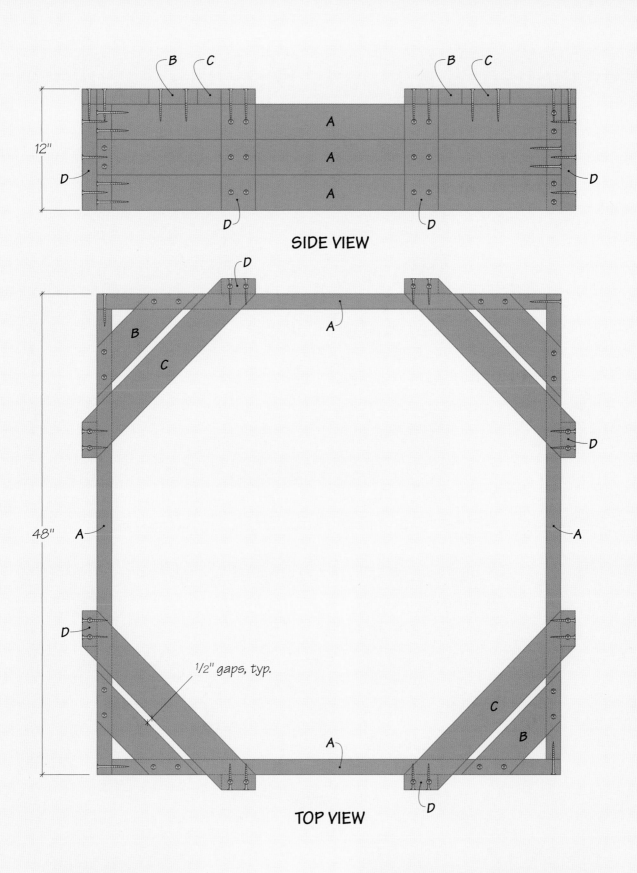

SIDE VIEW

12"

48"

1/2" gaps, typ.

TOP VIEW

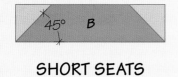

45° B

SHORT SEATS

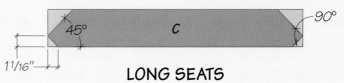

45° C 90°

1 1/16"

LONG SEATS

Frame-style Sandbox: Step-by-step

❶ Cut the 12 side tier pieces to length from 2 × 4 stock.

❷ Make the three tiers. Align the side pieces of each tier. Form the four butt joints on the tiers so that one end of each side piece overlaps the next side piece, while the other end is overlapped by the side piece before it. Assemble each tier, using countersunk 3-in. galvanized deck screws (**See Photo A**).

❸ Make the long seats. Cut the blanks to length, then measure

PHOTO A: Place the parts that compose each tier in position on your worksurface, alternating the orientation of the butt joints around the tier. Attach the parts with countersunk 3-in. galvanized deck screws. It's a good idea to wear gloves when working with treated lumber.

PHOTO B: Saw the long and short seat pieces to length, then miter-cut the ends to shape, according to the drawings shown on page 43. A power miter saw makes this task easy.

PHOTO C: Set a long seat on top of two braces, and drill countersunk pilot holes through the ends of the seat piece into the braces. Use 3-in. galvanized deck screws to secure the parts.

and mark the shape of the ends according to the *Long Seats* drawing on page 43. Cut the ends to shape with a power miter saw.

4 Make the short seats. Cut the blanks to length, then miter-cut the ends (**See Photo B**) to 45°.

5 Cut the eight braces to length.

6 Build four seat assemblies. Drill two countersunk pilot holes through the ends of each long seat, and fasten braces to the ends of the long seats with 3-in. galvanized deck screws (**See Photo C**).

7 Assemble the sandbox. Stack the completed tiers on top of each other, alternating the direction of the corner joints. Position the seat assemblies over the tier corners. Drill countersunk pilot holes through the braces, and fasten the braces to all three tiers by driving 2½-in. galvanized deck screws through the braces and into each tier (**See Photo D**).

8 Attach the short seats. Hold the ends flush with the outer face of the top tier. Drill countersunk pilot holes along the angled ends of the short seats, and fasten the seats with 3-in. deck screws.

FINISHING TOUCHES

9 Smooth the surfaces and ease corners and edges thoroughly with sandpaper, especially on and around the seats.

10 Finish the sandbox with latex primer and two coats of paint (**See Photo E**).

11 Position the sandbox. Line with landscape fabric to deter growth of unwanted vegetation. Fill the box with sand. TIP: *You'll need about 8 cubic ft. of sand.*

PHOTO D: Stack the three tiers with their corner joints alternating before installing the long seat assemblies. Secure the braces to the tiers with countersunk screws driven at every tier.

PHOTO E: Apply latex primer to all exposed surfaces of the sandbox, then follow up with two coats of exterior latex paint. We covered the whole box in a single color, but you could also create a multi-colored paint scheme instead.

Breezeway Boot Bench

This simple but elegant little bench will be equally at home in your breezeway, on your porch or even in your entryway. It's a great place to sit while
slipping boots on or off, bundling up the children or catching your breath after
that brisk walk. The hinged seat provides easy access to the inner ventilated
compartment with its aromatic cedar slatted bottom—a perfect place for
storing wet boots or extra shoes.

Vital Statistics: Breezeway Boot Bench

TYPE: Breezeway boot bench

OVERALL SIZE: 36½W by 21¼D by 32H

MATERIAL: White oak, aromatic cedar

JOINERY: Butt joints reinforced with screws and nails

CONSTRUCTION DETAILS:
- Bench front and back comprised of multiple panels spaced apart to improve air ventilation
- Bench bottom made of slatted cedar to promote drainage
- Seat mounted on piano hinge to provide access to inner storage compartment

FINISHING OPTIONS: Stain topcoated with penetrating UV protectant sealer

Building time

PREPARING STOCK
1-2 hours

LAYOUT
2-3 hours

CUTTING PARTS
3-5 hours

ASSEMBLY
5-8 hours

FINISHING
3-4 hours

TOTAL: 14-22 hours

Tools you'll use

- Table saw
- Jointer
- Jig saw
- Drill/driver
- ⅜-in.-dia. plug cutter
- Clamps
- Combination square
- Pneumatic nail gun or hammer and nailset
- Flush-trimming saw

Shopping list

- ☐ (1) 5/4 × 6 in. × 8 ft. white oak
- ☐ (2) 5/4 × 6 in. × 6 ft. white oak
- ☐ (1) 5/4 × 4 in. × 6 ft. white oak
- ☐ (1) 5/4 × 3 in. × 4 ft. white oak
- ☐ (2) 3/4 × 5½ in. × 6 ft. white oak
- ☐ (2) 3/4 × 1½ in. × 8 ft. white oak
- ☐ (1) 3/4 × 6 in. × 6 ft. aromatic cedar
- ☐ Flathead wood screws (1¼-, 2-in.)
- ☐ 1¼-in. finish nails
- ☐ 1½ × 36-in. brass-plated piano hinge, brass screws
- ☐ Wood glue
- ☐ Finishing materials

Breezeway Boot Bench

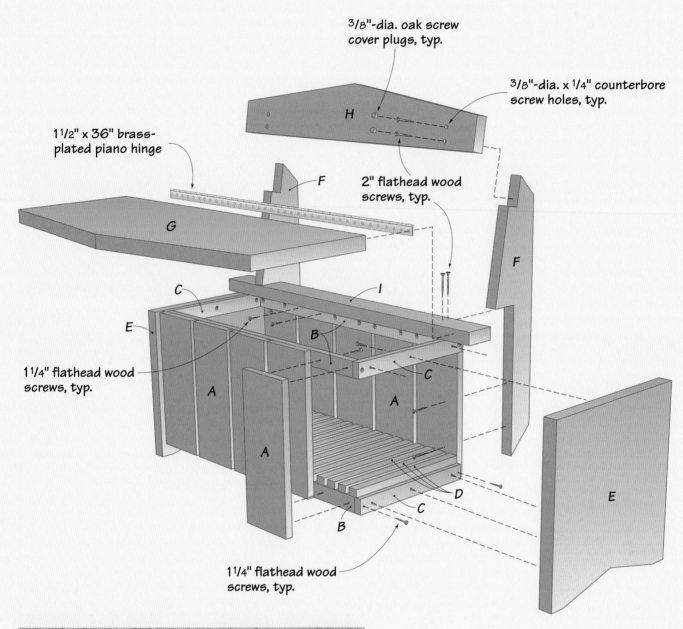

3/8"-dia. oak screw cover plugs, typ.

3/8"-dia. x 1/4" counterbore screw holes, typ.

1 1/2" x 36" brass-plated piano hinge

2" flathead wood screws, typ.

1 1/4" flathead wood screws, typ.

1 1/4" flathead wood screws, typ.

Breezeway Boot Bench Cutting List			
Part	No.	Size	Material
A. Front/back slats	10	$3/4 \times 5 1/2 \times 14$ in.	White oak
B. Long cleats	4	$3/4 \times 1 1/2 \times 29$ in.	"
C. Short cleats	4	$3/4 \times 1 1/2 \times 13 1/2$ in.	"
D. Bottom slats	20	$3/4 \times 1 \times 13 1/2$ in.	Aromatic cedar
E. Sides	2	$1 1/4 \times 15 1/4 \times 15 1/2$ in.	White oak
F. Back supports	2	$1 1/4 \times 5 1/2 \times 27 3/4$ in.	"
G. Seat	1	$1 1/4 \times 15 1/4 \times 36 1/2$ in.	"
H. Back rest	1	$1 1/4 \times 5 1/2 \times 33 1/2$ in.	"
I. Fixed seat slat	1	$1 1/4 \times 3 \times 36 1/2$ in.	"

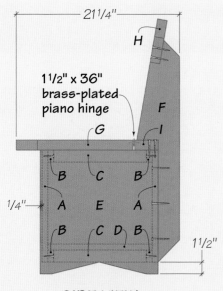

21 1/4"

H

1 1/2" x 36"
brass-plated
piano hinge

F

G

I

B   C   B

1/4"

A   E   A

B   C D B

1 1/2"

SIDE VIEW

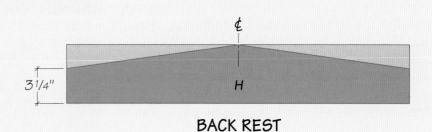

32"

H

F

3"

F

1/2" gaps, typ.

G

2 3/4"

1 3/4"

16 3/4"

A   A   A   A   A

E

D

E

FRONT VIEW

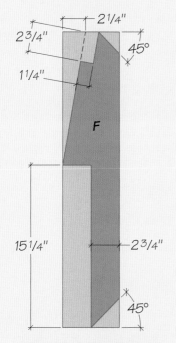

2 1/4"

2 3/4"

45°

1 1/4"

F

15 1/4"

2 3/4"

45°

BACK SUPPORTS

¢

3 1/4"

H

BACK REST

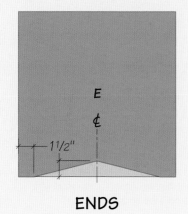

E

¢

1 1/2"

ENDS

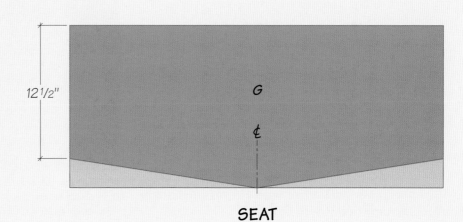

12 1/2"

G

¢

SEAT

MAKE THE FRONT & BACK PANELS

❶ Make the front and back slats. Cut the ten slats to length from 1 × 6 white oak stock, and sand the ends smooth. Cut the long and short cleats to length using 1 × 2 stock.

❷ Build the front and back panels. Cut four spacers, ½ × ¾ × 13½ in., and clamp them between five slats that will make up one side. NOTE: *The reason for cutting the spacers 13½ in. long is so they are ready to use again when installing the bottom slats.* Be sure the ends of the slats are flush. Position two long cleats flush with the top and bottom edges of the slats, and double-check that the cleats are ¼ in. short at each end. Drill countersunk pilot holes for attaching the cleats to the slats. Drive 1¼-in. flathead wood screws through the cleats into the slats (**See Photo A**). Repeat this process to build the other panel.

ASSEMBLE THE BENCH STRUCTURE

❸ Fasten the front and back panels together. Set the short cleats between the front and back panels so the ends of the short cleats fit into the ¼-in. notches formed by the long cleats and front and back panels. The top and bottom edges of the long and short cleats are flush. Drill a countersunk pilot hole at each end of the short cleats, and drive 1½-in. screws through the short cleats into the ends of the long cleats.

❹ Make the bottom slats. Rip four 6-ft.-long 1-in.-wide strips from the 6-ft. cedar 1 × 6. Crosscut the 20 slats to length with a miter saw or radial arm saw.

❺ Attach the bottom slats. Position the bottom slats evenly along the bottom of the bench on top of the long and short cleats, using the ½-in. spacers you made in Step 2 to space the slats. Fasten the slats with a pneumatic nail gun or with 1¼-in. finish nails and a hammer (**See Photo B**).

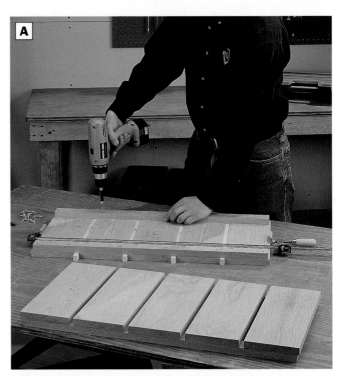

PHOTO A: Assemble the front and back panels by attaching pairs of long cleats to groups of five slats. Use spacers between the slats to hold them apart ½ in. Attach the cleats to the spacers with countersunk screws.

PHOTO B: Nail the cedar bottom slats to the top edges of the long and short cleats to form the bench bottom. Separate the slats with ½-in.-thick spacers as you fasten the slats in place.

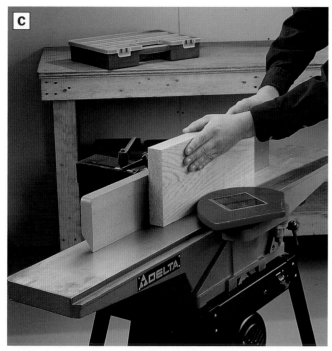

PHOTO C: Flatten the edges of the workpieces that will make up the side panels on the jointer or with a hand plane. Unless the boards are perfectly flat, gaps will show when you glue up the side panels.

PHOTO D: Glue and clamp up two side panels, alternating the clamps top and bottom to distribute clamping pressure. If the boards are cut longer than necessary, don't worry if the ends don't align at this stage.

MAKE THE SIDES

To get the width needed for the side panels, you'll need to edge-glue narrower stock. The 6-ft.-long, $5/4$ oak boards specified in the *Shopping List* are for this purpose. In general, attractive glued-up panels take a little planning. When selecting stock, look for similar color and grain pattern, or else plan the joint lines to highlight natural differences in the wood as a decorative element, by placing a darker or tighter grained piece between two equally sized lighter pieces. Always make sure that the glued-up panel is at least $1/2$ in. longer and wider than the finished piece you need, so you can trim it final size. You may want to trim the panel some on both sides to balance the wood grain pattern.

6 Cut pieces for the side panels to rough length ($1/2$ to 1 in. longer than final length), then flatten the edges on a jointer **(See Photo C)**. You could also smooth the edges with a hand plane.

7 Glue up the side panels. Spread wood glue along the mating edges of the boards, and clamp the boards together **(See Photo D)**. Alternate the clamps above and below the panels to prevent bowing, and don't overtighten the clamps or you'll squeeze out too much glue. It is best not to wipe up the excess glue while it's wet, because it will clog the pores of the surrounding wood and show up dramatically when the

PHOTO E: Set the side panels into position on the short cleats, so the front edges of the sides overhang the bench front by $1/4$ in. and the tops of the sides are flush with the top cleats. Screw through the short cleats to attach the sides to the bench.

PHOTO F: Cut the back supports, back rest and seat to shape, using the detail drawings on page 49 as a guide for establishing the profiles.

PHOTO G: Insert thin spacers between the fixed seat slat and the seat to provide for hinge clearance. Clamp the parts and install the hinge.

piece is stained. Leave lines of squeezed-out glue until they partially dry, then slice them off cleanly with a sharp chisel. When the panels are dry, sand the joints smooth.

8 Cut the two sides to 15¼ in. long and 15½ in. wide. Use the *Ends* drawing, page 49, to mark the V-shaped profile on the bottoms of the side panels, and cut out the profiles with a jig saw.

9 Attach the sides to the bench structure. To do this, you'll screw from inside the bench through the short cleats. Extend the side panels ¼ in. beyond the front of the bench. Fasten through the upper short cleats first, keeping the top edges of the side panels flush with the top edges of the cleats. Drill countersunk pilot holes, and attach the parts with 1¼-in. flathead wood screws. Then fasten the lower short cleats to the sides (**See Photo E**).

MAKE & INSTALL THE BACK REST & SEAT
10 Make the back supports. Cut the blanks to size from 6-in.-wide ⁵⁄₄ oak stock. Refer to the *Back Supports* drawing, page 49, for laying out the shape of the back supports on your workpieces. Cut out the parts and sand the cut edges smooth.

11 Make the back rest. Cut the blank to length, mark the sloped profile using the *Back Rest* drawing on page 49 and cut out the part with a jig saw.

12 Cut the fixed seat slat to length, using the piece of 3-in.-wide, ⁵⁄₄ oak stock specified in the *Shopping List,* page 47.

13 Make the seat. Cut, edge-joint and glue up stock for a seat blank. Mark the angled profile on the front edge of the seat. Clamp the seat to your worksurface, and cut out the final shape with a jig saw (**See Photo F**). Sand the cut edges smooth.

14 Install the piano hinge. Position the fixed seat slat face down along the back edge of the seat. Cut spacers that match the combined thickness of the two hinge leaves, and insert the spacers between the seat and the slat. Clamp the slat and seat together with their ends flush. Center the hinge so the hinge knuckle aligns with the spacers, drill pilot holes and attach the hinge to the slat and seat with screws (**See Photo G**).

15 Attach the seat assembly to the bench. Position the seat assembly on the bench structure with the back edge of the fixed seat slat flush with the back of the bench. The ends of the seat assembly should overhang the bench sides by 1¾ in. On the seat slat, mark the locations where the back supports will overlap. Drill countersunk pilot holes in these areas. Fasten the seat assembly to the bench by screwing through the fixed slat down into the upper back long cleat and the ends of the back slats (**See Photo H**).

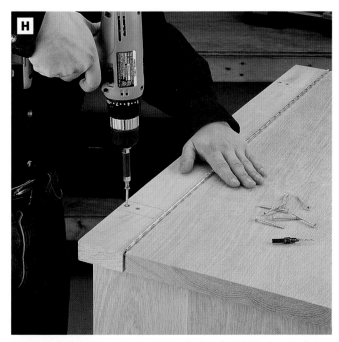

PHOTO H: Fasten the seat assembly to the bench, driving countersunk wood screws in the areas on the fixed seat slat that will be covered by the back supports. Screw into the upper long cleats and back slats.

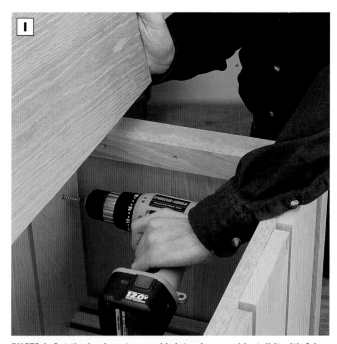

PHOTO I: Set the back rest assembly into place, and install it with 2-in. flathead wood screws driven through the back slats and into the back supports. Measure carefully when establishing screw locations.

16 Assemble the back rest. Measure in from the ends of the back rest and draw guidelines on the face at 3⅝ in. Clamp the back rest into the top notches of the back supports, with the supports centered on these guidelines. Drill countersunk pilot holes through the back rest and into the supports. Counterbore the holes ¼ in. to accommodate wood plugs. Screw the back rest to the supports.

17 Attach the back rest assembly to the bench. Clamp the assembly in place, drill countersunk pilot holes through the back slats into the supports, and fasten the parts with 2-in. flathead wood screws (**See Photo I**).

FINISHING TOUCHES

18 Plug the screw holes. Use a plug cutter to cut ⅜-in. oak plugs, apply glue, and tap the plugs into place with a wooden mallet. You could use wood filler or dowel pieces instead of wood plugs, if you prefer. Trim the plugs flush and sand smooth (**See Photo J**).

19 Sand all surfaces, edges and corners well. Stain the bench as you like, and topcoat with sealer or varnish.

PHOTO J: Install wood plugs or use an oak-tinted wood filler to cover screws used to attach the back rest to the back supports. Generally, wood plugs are easier to conceal because they blend in better with the surrounding wood surfaces. Trim the plugs with a flush-cutting saw (if necessary), and sand these areas thoroughly.

Picnic Table & Benches

A good old-fashioned picnic table with matching benches is almost as all-American as baseball and apple pie. What yard or deck is complete without one? Our version of this classic is just a notch dressier than many similar pieces because it is designed with no visible screws in the table or bench surfaces, and the outer edges are neatly rounded over.

Vital Statistics: Picnic Table & Benches

TYPE: Picnic table and benches

OVERALL SIZE: Table: 37¼W by 71L by 29½H
Benches: 11W by 71L by 16½H

MATERIAL: Cedar

JOINERY: Butt joints reinforced with galvanized screws

CONSTRUCTION DETAILS:
· Butt joint construction
· No exposed screw heads in tabletop or bench surfaces
· Angled table braces allow for comfortable leg room
· Bench legs tuck between table legs for compact storage

FINISHING OPTIONS: Penetrating UV protectant sealer, exterior paint or leave unfinished to weather to gray

Building time

PREPARING STOCK
0 hours

LAYOUT
1-3 hours

CUTTING PARTS
2-4 hours

ASSEMBLY
3-5 hours

FINISHING
2-3 hours

TOTAL: 8-15 hours

Tools you'll use

· Circular saw or power miter saw
· Router with ½-in. roundover bit
· Jig saw
· Drill/driver
· Clamps
· Sockets
· Combination square
· Bevel gauge

Shopping list

☐ (5) 2 × 8 in. × 6 ft. cedar
☐ (3) 2 × 6 in. × 8 ft. cedar
☐ (3) 2 × 6 in. × 6 ft. cedar
☐ (5) 2 × 4 in. × 8 ft. cedar
☐ Galvanized deck screws (2½-in.)
☐ Galvanized lag bolts (¼ × 4½-in.)
☐ Finishing materials

Picnic Table & Benches

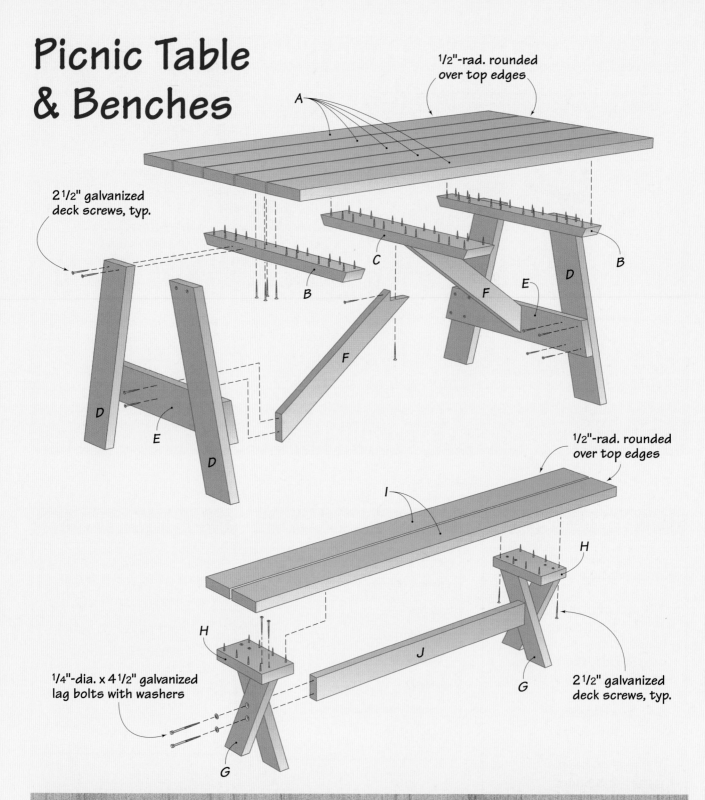

1/2"-rad. rounded over top edges

A

2 1/2" galvanized deck screws, typ.

B

C

B

D

E

F

E

D

B

F

D

1/2"-rad. rounded over top edges

I

H

H

J

G

G

1/4"-dia. x 4 1/2" galvanized lag bolts with washers

2 1/2" galvanized deck screws, typ.

Picnic Table & Benches Cutting List

Part	No.	Size	Material	Part	No.	Size	Material
A. Table slats	5	$1 1/2 \times 7 1/4 \times 71$ in.	Cedar	**F.** Angled braces	2	$1 1/2 \times 3 1/2 \times 31 3/8$ in.	Cedar
B. Outer stretchers	2	$1 1/2 \times 3 1/2 \times 34 1/4$ in.	"	**G.** Bench legs	8	$1 1/2 \times 3 1/2 \times 16 3/4$ in.	"
C. Center stretcher	1	$1 1/2 \times 5 1/2 \times 34 1/4$ in.	"	**H.** Bench stretchers	4	$1 1/2 \times 5 1/2 \times 10 1/2$ in.	"
D. Table legs	4	$1 1/2 \times 5 1/2 \times 30 1/2$ in.	"	**I.** Bench slats	4	$1 1/2 \times 5 1/2 \times 71$ in.	"
E. Leg braces	2	$1 1/2 \times 5 1/2 \times 33$ in.	"	**J.** Bench braces	2	$1 1/2 \times 3 1/2 \times 42$ in.	"

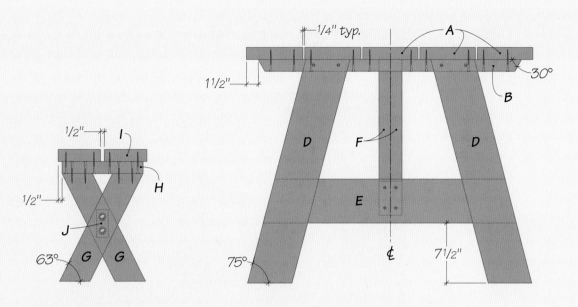

BENCH END VIEW　　　　**TABLE END VIEW**

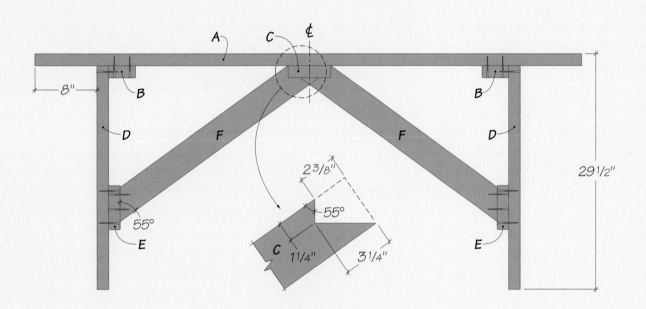

TABLE FRONT VIEW

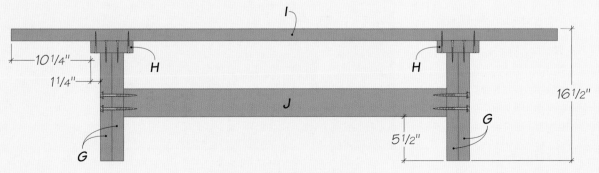

BENCH FRONT VIEW

PHOTO A: Clamp the tabletop slats together and rout the ends and edges with a ½-in. roundover bit. Clamping the slats together will produce an even profile on the ends of the slats.

BUILD THE TABLETOP

1 Crosscut the five table slats to length from 2 × 8 stock.

2 Round over the outside edges and ends of the table slats. Clamp the slats together, faceup, with the ends flush. Use your router and a ½-in. roundover bit to ease the ends of the slats and the edges of the outer slats (**See Photo A**). Unclamp the slats.

3 Mark the three stretcher locations on the table slats. Turn the slats facedown and clamp the slats together again with their ends flush. Mark the locations of the outer and center stretchers. The center stretcher is centered on the length of the slats. The outer stretchers are 9½ in. from each end of the tabletop. Extend the stretcher layout lines across the slats with a carpenter's square.

4 Measure and cut the stretchers to length, with the ends beveled at a 30° angle (**See Photo B**).

5 Fasten the stretchers to the table slats. To do this, first insert ¼-in.-thick scrap spacers between the slats to hold them evenly apart. Set the stretchers in place. Drill countersunk pilot holes, and attach the stretchers to the slats with 2½-in. galvanized deck screws (**See Photo C**).

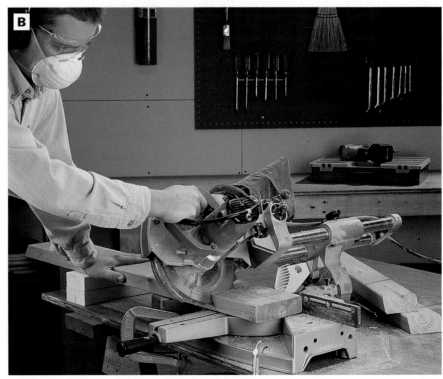

PHOTO B: Bevel-cut the ends of the outer and center table stretchers at 30° angles. We used a power miter box, but you could also make these cuts with a circular saw or a table saw.

BUILD THE LEG ASSEMBLIES

6 Crosscut the four table legs to length. If you are using a radial arm saw or a power miter saw, clamp a stop to the saw's fence to ensure that the legs are cut exactly to the same length. Cut the ends of each leg to 75°.

7 Cut the two leg braces to length and trim the ends to 75°.

8 Attach the braces to the legs. Use a square to establish a mark 7½ in. up from the bottom end of each leg (See *Table End View*, page 57). Set a bevel gauge to 75° and use the gauge to draw a line across this mark so the line is parallel to the ends of the leg. Position a brace on each pair of legs, holding the ends of the brace flush with the outer edges of the legs. Drill four countersunk pilot holes through the leg braces and into the legs. Fasten the parts with deck screws (**See Photo D**).

ASSEMBLE THE TABLE

9 Cut the two angled braces. First crosscut the braces to length from 2 × 4 stock. Next, cut a 55° angle on the lower ends. Then, refer to the *Table Front View* detail drawing on page 57 to mark the "birdsmouth" notches on the upper ends of the braces. Clamp each brace to your worksurface, and cut out these notches with a jig saw (**See Photo E**).

10 Attach the leg assemblies to the tabletop. Drill a pair of countersunk pilot holes in the top end of each leg. Stand the leg assemblies in place against the outside edges of the outer stretchers on the tabletop. Be sure the leg braces face in toward the center of the table. Drive 2½-in. galvanized deck screws through the legs into the tabletop stretchers.

PHOTO C: Mark locations for the three table stretchers on the bottom of the tabletop, then fasten the stretchers to the table slats with 2½-in. galvanized deck screws. Set ¼-in. spacers between the slats before you fasten the stretchers to keep the slats held evenly apart.

PHOTO D: Cut the legs and leg braces to size, and cut the ends of the parts at 75° angles. Use the *Table End View* drawing, page 57, as a reference for cutting the parts. Then construct the two table leg assemblies by fastening each leg brace to a pair of legs with deck screws.

PHOTO E: Cut birdsmouth notches on the upper ends of the angled braces with a jig saw so the braces will interlock with the center table stretcher. Clamp each brace to your worksurface to hold it steady while you make the cuts.

PHOTO F: Fasten the leg assemblies to the outer stretchers, then attach the angled braces to the center stretcher and leg braces. The parts will be easiest to manage if you work with the tabletop turned upside down on sawhorses.

⓫ Attach the angled braces. Mark a centerline across the width of the center stretcher. Position the birdsmouth ends of the angled braces on either side of this centerline, so the angled braces flare out to the leg braces. Drill countersunk pilot holes, and attach the angled braces to the center stretcher with 2½-in. deck screws **(See Photo F)**. Use a carpenter's square to adjust each angled brace so it is square with the leg brace. Attach the angled braces to the leg braces by holding each one in position, drilling countersunk pilot holes, and fastening the parts with 2½-in. deck screws. Drive the screws through the leg braces and into the angled braces.

BUILD THE BENCH LEG ASSEMBLIES

⓬ Cut the eight bench legs to length, then trim the ends to 63°. Temporarily fasten pairs of legs together with a single deck screw where the legs cross to form four "X"-shaped leg assemblies. Attach the legs together so the overall measurement at the top of the "X" is 10½ in. NOTE: *The screw will make it possible to adjust the "X" formed by the legs in or out so the bottoms of the legs stand flat.* Take care to position these temporary screws so that they don't interfere with the lag screws that will be used later to attach the leg assemblies to the bench braces.

⓭ Fasten the four bench stretchers to the leg pairs. Cut the stretchers to length. Draw a centerline along the length of each stretcher. When you attach the bench stretchers to the legs, align the inside faces of the legs along the stretcher centerlines. Adjust the legs in or out until they rest flat against the bottom of the stretcher. Check to be sure the legs also stand flat at the bottom. Fasten the stretchers to the legs with deck screws (See Photo G).

ASSEMBLE THE BENCHES

14 Cut the bench slats to length. Clamp pairs of slats together with the ends flush, and round over the top ends and edges of the slats as you did in Step 2 with a router and ½-in. roundover bit.

15 Attach the leg assemblies to the bench slats. Drill countersunk pilot holes through the stretchers from the underside. Lay the bench slats facedown on your worksurface. Mark the stretcher locations on the slats, 10¼ in. from each end. Set the leg assemblies in place on the bench slats, and space the slats apart so they overhang the ends of the stretchers by ½ in. Fasten the leg assemblies by driving 2½-in. deck screws through the stretchers and into the slats.

16 Install the bench braces. Cut the bench braces to length. Clamp each brace in place between the bench leg assemblies. Drill ⅜-in.-deep holes in the outermost legs to recess two lag screw heads using a ¾-in.-dia. spade bit. Then drill ¼-in.-dia. holes in the center of the counterbored recesses through the legs and into the braces. Drive pairs of 4½-in.-long lag screws and washers into place with a ratchet to fasten the legs to the braces **(See Photo H)**. Remove the temporary screws you installed in Step 12.

FINISHING TOUCHES

17 Sand all surfaces of the table and benches smooth. We applied a clear UV protectant exterior sealer to highlight the beauty of the cedar, but this project could be stained, painted or left to weather naturally.

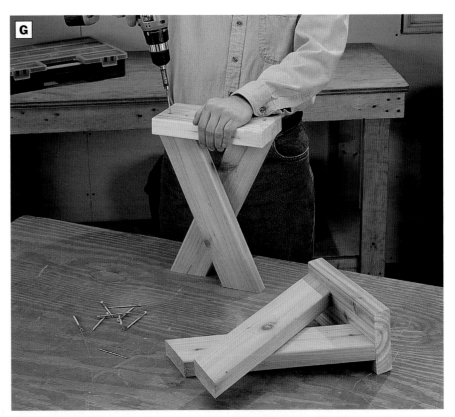

PHOTO G: Attach a bench stretcher to each pair of legs with screws. Align the top outer corners of the legs with the ends of the stretchers, and center the legs widthwise on the stretchers. NOTE: *Adjust the spread of the legs on the stretchers, if necessary, so the legs will stand flat.*

Clamp

PHOTO H: Cut the bench braces to length and clamp them in position 5½ in. from the bottoms of the legs on each bench. Drill ¾-in.-dia. counterbores in the outermost legs to recess two lag bolt heads, then drill pilot holes through the counterbored holes to install the lag bolts. Slip a washer onto each lag bolt before you screw it through the legs and into the bench braces.

Daytripper Chair

This two-part chair is made up of two interlocking and removable substructures that nestle one inside the other for easy storage or portability. When set up, it is as handsome as it is sturdy and comfortable. This chair will be equally at home on your deck, on the sidelines of the soccer field or in your living room, if you're ever in need of extra seating.

See pages 68-75 for plans on how to build a matching table to accompany this Daytripper Chair project. The table folds down to nearly flat for storage and transport.

Vital Statistics: Daytripper Chair

TYPE: Daytripper chair

OVERALL SIZE: 23W by 30L by 30½H

MATERIAL: Red oak, pressure-treated pine

JOINERY: Butt joints reinforced with galvanized deck screws

CONSTRUCTION DETAILS:
- Back and seat supports built from treated lumber for strength
- Oak plugs conceal screws in slats
- Handle integrated into top two back slats
- Chair disassembles for ease of storage and transport

FINISHING OPTIONS: Danish oil or a penetrating UV protectant sealer, exterior latex paint

Building time

PREPARING STOCK
0 hours

LAYOUT
1-2 hours

CUTTING PARTS
1-2 hours

ASSEMBLY
4-6 hours

FINISHING
2-3 hours

TOTAL: 8-13 hours

Tools you'll use

- Band saw or jig saw
- Circular saw or power miter saw
- Router with ⅛-in. roundover bit, ½-in. straight bit
- Drill/driver
- Drill press
- ⅜-in. plug cutter
- Compass
- Mallet
- Clamps

Shopping list

- ☐ (1) ¾ × 10 in. × 8 ft. pressure-treated pine
- ☐ (1) ¾ × 8 in. × 8 ft. pressure-treated pine
- ☐ (2) ¾ × 4¾ in. × 8 ft. red oak
- ☐ Galvanized deck screws (1½-in.)
- ☐ Moisture-resistant wood glue
- ☐ Danish oil or penetrating UV protectant sealer
- ☐ Latex primer
- ☐ Exterior latex paint

Daytripper Chair

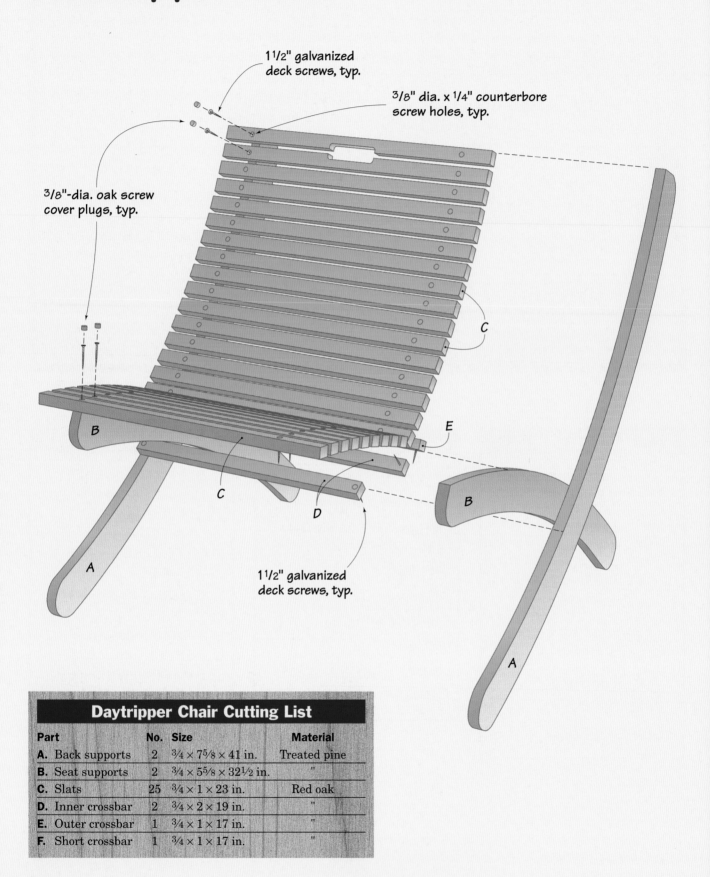

1 1/2" galvanized deck screws, typ.

3/8" dia. x 1/4" counterbore screw holes, typ.

3/8"-dia. oak screw cover plugs, typ.

B

C

A

E

C

D

1 1/2" galvanized deck screws, typ.

B

A

Daytripper Chair Cutting List

Part	No.	Size	Material
A. Back supports	2	$3/4 \times 7\,5/8 \times 41$ in.	Treated pine
B. Seat supports	2	$3/4 \times 5\,5/8 \times 32\,1/2$ in.	"
C. Slats	25	$3/4 \times 1 \times 23$ in.	Red oak
D. Inner crossbar	2	$3/4 \times 2 \times 19$ in.	"
E. Outer crossbar	1	$3/4 \times 1 \times 17$ in.	"
F. Short crossbar	1	$3/4 \times 1 \times 17$ in.	"

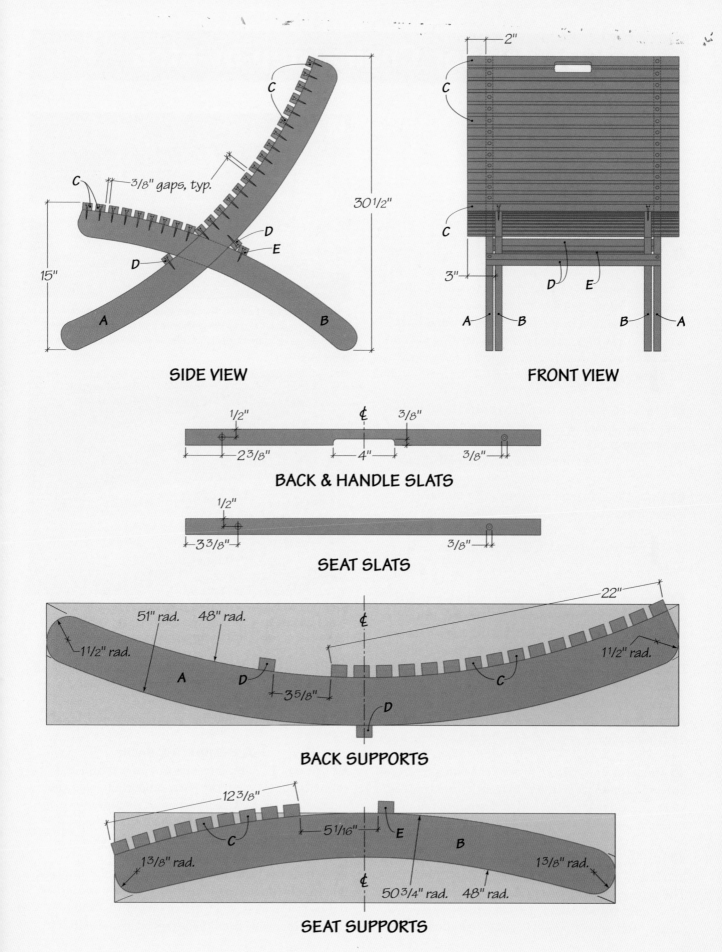

SIDE VIEW

FRONT VIEW

BACK & HANDLE SLATS

SEAT SLATS

BACK SUPPORTS

SEAT SUPPORTS

PHOTO A: Create seat and back support templates from hardboard, and use these templates to draw the profiles on the back and seat support workpieces (use treated lumber, not plywood as shown). Cut out the parts with a jig saw.

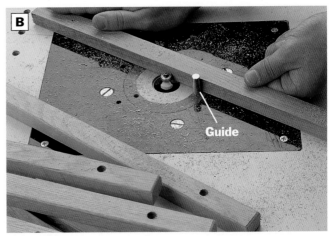

PHOTO B: Ease the edges and ends of the slats and crossbars with a ⅛-in. roundover bit in the router table. Use a pin-style guide on the router table to help control the workpieces as you machine them.

CUT OUT THE PARTS

❶ Cut two back supports and two seat supports to size and shape. To ensure identical pairs, use templates made from ¼-in. hardboard to trace profiles onto the workpieces **(See Photo A)**. Follow the dimensions shown in the *Back Supports* and *Seat Supports* drawings, page 65. Before cutting out the back supports, measure and mark the centerline to use later as a reference line for crossbar installation.

❷ Paint the supports. Sand the surfaces and edges well. Apply a coat of latex primer, then two coats of exterior latex paint. Transfer the centerline reference mark on the back supports to the painted surfaces.

❸ Make the slats and crossbars. Cut blanks to length from ¾-in. oak stock. Set the fence on your table saw to rip the 1-in.-wide slats and crossbars. Re-set the fence to cut the 2-in.-wide, inner long crossbar.

❹ Drill counterbored pilot holes in the back slats and seat slats for attaching these parts to the supports later. Designate 16 slats as the back slats and the remaining nine slats for the seat. Drill a pilot hole 2⅜ in. from each end of the back slats, so the counterbore portion of each hole is ⅜ in. deep. This is easiest to do using a depth setting on a drill press. At the same drill press depth setting, drill a pilot hole 3⅜ in. from each end of the seat slats.

❺ Make the crossbars. Crosscut the two long crossbars and the short crossbar to length from the 1-in. stock you ripped in Step 3. Drill counterbored pilot holes for screws ⅜ in. from each end.

❻ Rout a ⅛-in. roundover on the edges and ends of one face of the slats and crossbars **(See Photo B)**. The proportions of these parts are too narrow to rout "freehand" with a router, so shape these parts on a router table with a pin-style guide installed.

❼ Rout a "handle" in the adjoining edges of two back slats (See *Back & Handle Slats*, page 65), using a ½-in. straight bit in the router table and cutting a ⅜ × 4-in. centered notch in both slats **(See Photo C)**.

ASSEMBLE THE BACK

❽ Cut two 17½-in.-long spacers from scrap, and clamp them between the back supports to hold the supports in place. Use a carpenter's square to verify that the ends of the supports are even with one another. Set the assembly concave-side-up.

❾ Attach the back slats. Screw the top slat in place, holding the upper edge flush with the top corners of the back supports and the handle profile facing inward. Measure from the attached slat (See *Back*

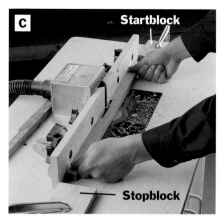

PHOTO C: Make handle cutouts in two back slats using a router table and straight bit. Install start- and stopblocks to limit the length of cut when routing these recesses.

PHOTO D: When installing the back and seat slats to the supports, clamp scrap spacers between the supports to keep them aligned.

PHOTO E: Cover exposed screw heads on the slats and crossbars with oak plugs. Glue and insert the plugs, trim them and sand smooth.

Supports drawing, page 65) and mark the location of the lowest back slat. Screw this slat in place.

10 Verify the spacing of the remaining back slats between the top and bottom slats (about ½ in.). Attach these 15 back slats with 1½-in. galvanized deck screws, starting from the top with the slat that completes the handle cutout.

11 Install the inner long crossbar. Measure 3⅝ in. from the lowest back slat to position the crossbar. Screw the crossbar in place.

ASSEMBLE THE SEAT
12 Follow the same procedure as for the back assembly. Cut two spacers 15½ in. long, and clamp them between the seat supports.

13 Screw the front seat slat in place, with the edge flush with the top corners of the seat supports.

14 Measure 12⅜ in. from the attached seat slat, and mark the location of the last seat slat. Screw this slat in place.

15 Verify the spacing of the remaining seat slats (approximately ⅜ in.), and attach the rest of the slats with 1½-in. galvanized deck screws **(See Photo D)**.

ASSEMBLE THE CHAIR
16 Plug all of the screw holes. Cut ⅜-in.-dia. oak plugs with a plug cutter. Glue and tap the plugs into place **(See Photo E)**. Trim and sand the plugs flush.

17 Attach the outer long crossbar in place on the back support centerline you drew in Step 1.

18 Slide the seat into position between the back supports. Use C-clamps at the intersections of the supports to hold the two assemblies in place. Mark the correct locations for the short crossbar **(See Photo F)**. It should rest against the outer long crossbar. Attach the crossbar with galvanized deck screws. Then plug, trim and sand the crossbar screw holes.

FINISHING TOUCHES
19 Break all edges on the raw oak parts thoroughly with sandpaper. Mask off the painted surfaces of the supports, and cover the slats with Danish oil or a UV protectant sealer.

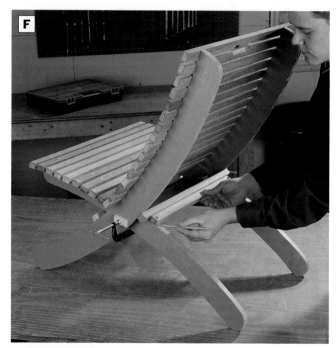

PHOTO F: Slide the seat assembly into the back assembly and use C-clamps to hold the chair together. Set the short crossbar against the lower long crossbar, mark its position, and install it with screws.

Daytripper Table

This folding table goes anywhere and stores easily, yet it has the look of fine furniture. Its contrasting base and top and its neatly plugged screw holes highlight both stylishness in conception and craftsmanship in construction. You can easily alter this versatile design to suit your decor by simply changing the species of wood for the top slats, the color of paint on the table subassembly or both.

See pages 62-67 for plans on how to build a matching chair to complement this Daytripper Table project. The chair pulls apart into two sections that nest one inside the other for storage.

Vital Statistics: Daytripper Table

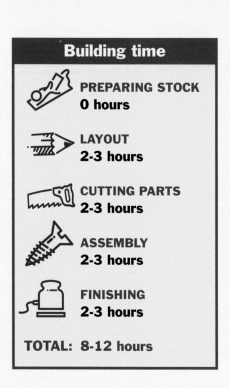

TYPE: Folding table

OVERALL SIZE: 16W by 22L by 16H

MATERIAL: Red oak, exterior plywood

JOINERY: Butt joints reinforced with galvanized deck screws

CONSTRUCTION DETAILS:
· Legs made of plywood for strength
· Screws concealed with matching wood plugs on oak parts
· Table folds flat by way of pivot dowels on the stretchers and legs

FINISHING OPTIONS: Penetrating UV protectant sealer, exterior latex paint

---

Building time

PREPARING STOCK
0 hours

LAYOUT
2-3 hours

CUTTING PARTS
2-3 hours

ASSEMBLY
2-3 hours

FINISHING
2-3 hours

TOTAL: 8-12 hours

Tools you'll use

· Band saw or jig saw
· Drill press
· Table saw
· Circular saw or power miter saw
· Compass
· Drill/driver
· Clamps

Shopping list

☐ (1) ³/4 in. × 4 × 4 ft. exterior plywood

☐ (1) ³/4 × 3¹/2 in. × 8 ft. red oak

☐ (2) ³/4-in.-dia. × 36-in. hardwood dowel

☐ (1) ¹/4-in.-dia. × 36-in. hardwood dowel

☐ Galvanized deck screws (1¹/2-in.)

☐ #6d galvanized finish nails

☐ UV protectant sealer

☐ Latex primer

☐ Exterior latex paint

Daytripper Table

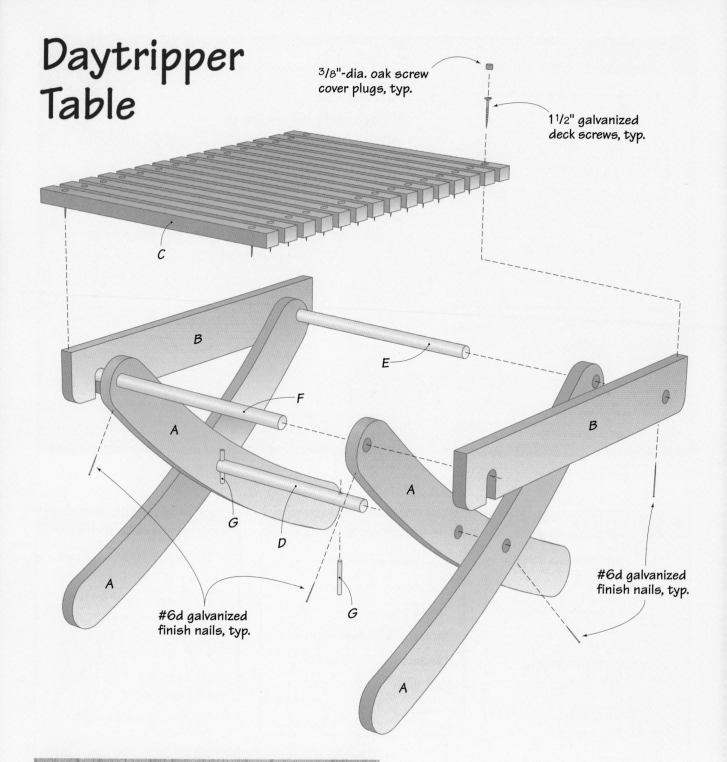

3/8"-dia. oak screw cover plugs, typ.

1 1/2" galvanized deck screws, typ.

C

B

E

A

F

G

D

A

B

A

A

G

#6d galvanized finish nails, typ.

#6d galvanized finish nails, typ.

Daytripper Table Cutting List			
Part	**No.**	**Size**	**Material**
A. Legs	4	$3/4 \times 4 1/4 \times 25$ in.	Exterior plywood
B. Stretchers	2	$3/4 \times 3 \times 21 1/2$ in.	"
C. Slats	15	$3/4 \times 1 \times 16$ in.	Oak
D. Leg pivot dowel	1	$3/4$ dia. $\times 12 7/16$ in.	Hardwood
E. Table pivot dowel	1	$3/4$ dia. $\times 14 1/8$ in.	"
F. Table lock dowel	1	$3/4$ dia. $\times 14 1/8$ in.	"
G. Lock dowels	2	$1/4$ dia. $\times 1 1/4$ in.	"

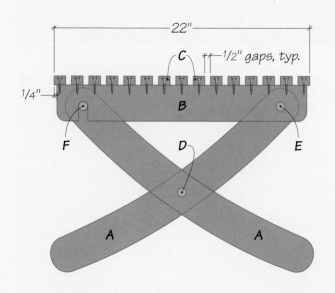

SIDE VIEW

END VIEW

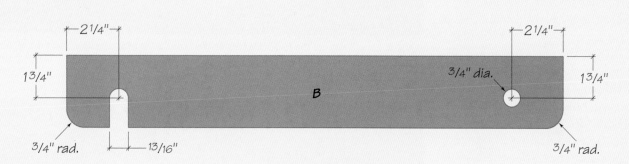

STRETCHERS

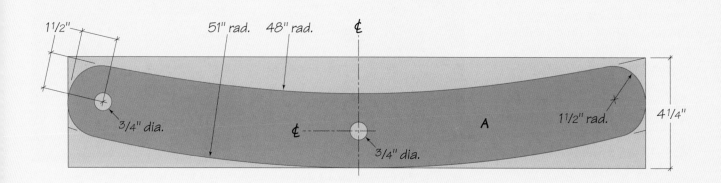

LEGS

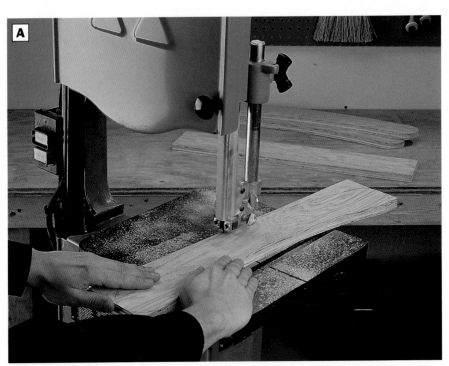

PHOTO A: Lay out and cut the four table legs on the band saw or with a jig saw. Since the profiles of the legs match, mark and cut one to serve as a template for tracing the profiles onto the other three leg blanks.

MAKE THE LEGS

1 Lay out one leg on a piece of ³/₄-in. exterior plywood, cut it to shape, and use it as a template for the other three legs. To lay out the leg, draw two 3-in.-dia. circles with their centerpoints 22 in. apart. Mark the midpoint between the circles with a perpendicular line, for use later in locating the hole for the leg pivot dowel. Clamp the workpiece to your workbench and extend the perpendicular line you just drew onto the benchtop. Use this line as the pivot point for connecting the circles with a 48-in.-radius arc for the inner curve of the leg and a 51-in.-radius arc for the outer curve (See the *Legs* drawing, page 71). Drill a ¹/₁₆-in. locater hole through the center-points of the two dowel holes in the leg. Cut out the leg and sand the cut edges smooth.

2 Trace the leg template onto three plywood leg blanks. Mark the centerpoints of the leg dowel holes by drilling through the locater holes in the template.

3 Cut out the legs (**See Photo A**), and sand the profiles smooth.

4 Drill the dowel holes in the legs (**See Photo B**). It is impor-tant that these holes be bored straight, so use a drill press or right-angle drill guide.

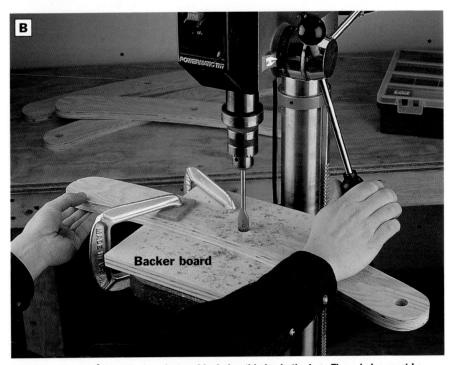

Backer board

PHOTO B: Bore the ³/₄-in.-dia. leg pivot and lock dowel holes in the legs. These holes must be drilled straight through the legs, or the dowels will be difficult to align during assembly. Bore the holes with a drill press, or mount your drill/driver in a right-angle drill guide. Set a backer board beneath each workpiece before you drill, to keep the bit from tearing out the wood as it exits.

Make the stretchers & slats

❺ Cut the stretchers to size and shape. Start by cutting two plywood blanks to length and width. Mark the centerpoints of the pivot dowel hole and the hole that will form the base of the lock dowel slot on each stretcher (See *Stretchers* drawing, page 71). Draw the ¾-in. radiused corners and cut them with your jig saw.

❻ Drill the dowel holes. Note that the diameter of the hole that will become the slot for the table lock dowel is ¹³⁄₁₆ in., so that the lock dowel can move freely in and out of the slot. Use a drill press or right-angle drill guide to bore these holes as straight as possible.

❼ Cut the lock dowel slots in the stretchers (**See Photo C**). Use a combination square to draw lines from the outer edges of the ¹³⁄₁₆-in. lock dowel hole to the edge of the stretcher with the curved corners. Clamp the stretcher to your worksurface, and cut along the lines to make the slots.

❽ Finish the legs and stretchers. Fill any voids in the edges of the plywood with wood putty or auto body filler. Sand the parts smooth. Prime the legs and stretchers with a high-quality latex primer. After the primer dries, apply two coats of exterior latex paint.

❾ Make the slats. Crosscut six 16-in.-long blanks from red oak stock. Set the fence on your table saw 1 in. from the blade, and rip the 15 slats to width.

❿ Drill counterbored pilot holes in the slats. Make a right-angle jig for your drill press to index placement of the screw holes. Clamp the jig in place so the pilot holes are centered on the slats and inset

PHOTO C: Connect the lock dowel hole with straight lines to the edge of each stretcher, forming the lock dowel slots. Clamp the legs to your worksurface and cut along these lines. The width of the slots should be ¹³⁄₁₆ in., to provide a loose fit for the ¾-in.-dia. lock dowel.

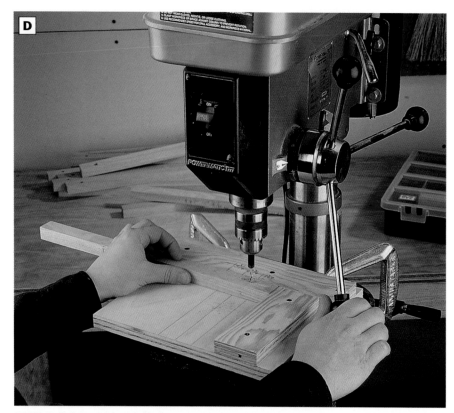

PHOTO D: Build a right-angle jig from scrap to help index placement of the counterbored holes in the ends of the slats. Clamp the jig to the drill press table so each slat is exactly aligned for drilling when you lay it in the jig. This way, there's no need to measure and mark each slat hole.

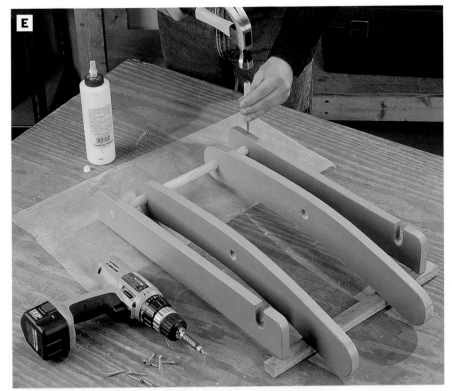

PHOTO E: Attach the first tabletop slat to the stretchers with screws. Lay the outer legs between the stretchers, and slide the table pivot dowel through the stretchers and outer legs. Pin the dowel in place with glue and finish nails driven into the dowel through the stretchers. Do not glue or nail the outer legs to the table pivot dowel.

PHOTO F: Install the inner legs between the outer legs, and insert the leg pivot dowel through the center dowel holes in the legs. Cut and insert the table lock dowel through the inner legs. Pin the table lock dowel to the inner legs and the leg pivot dowel to the outer legs with finish nails.

$1^3/8$ in. from the ends (See Photo D). Set the depth stop on the drill press so the counterbored portion of the holes is ¼ in. deep, to allow for inserting wood plugs later.

⑪ Round over the edges and ends on one face of all the slats. The quickest method for doing this is to use a ⅛-in. piloted roundover bit in the router table. Or, you could ease these edges and ends with a sander instead.

ASSEMBLE THE TABLE

⑫ Attach the first slat to the stretchers to help establish their alignment during assembly. Start at the end with the lock dowel slot. Position the slat so it over-hangs the outside faces of the stretchers by 1 in. and the ends of the stretchers by ¼ in. Fasten the slat in place with 1½-in. gal-vanized deck screws.

⑬ Install the table pivot dowel. Cut the dowel to length, and slip it through the end holes in the outer legs and stretchers. Assemble the parts so the concave profiles of the outer legs will face the tabletop slats. Fasten the dowel with glue and a #6d galvanized finish nail driven through each stretcher (See Photo E). Drill 1/16-in. pilot holes before driving the nails. Once fastened, the pivot dowel holds the tabletop frame in shape.

⑭ Attach the remaining table slats with screws. Start with the other end slat, overhanging it ¼ in. beyond the ends of the stretchers. Space the 13 interme-diate slats ½ in. apart, with all ends lined up. Use spacers to help establish even gaps as you attach the slats.

⑮ Install the inner legs. With the table facedown on your worksurface, position the inner legs by setting them concave-side-down between the outer legs and sliding the leg pivot dowel through the center dowel holes in the legs.

⓰ Cut and fasten the table lock dowel to the inner legs. Space the inner legs by sliding them lightly against the inner faces of the outer legs. Insert the lock dowel through the end holes in the inner legs and position it so there is an equal overhang on each side. Fasten the lock dowel by drilling a pilot hole through the end of each leg and driving a finish nail into the dowel.

⓱ Fasten the leg pivot dowel. Drill a pilot hole into each outer leg, and drive a finish nail through the pilot hole into the dowel (See Photo F).

⓲ Install lock dowels through the leg pivot dowel. The lock dowels hold the inner legs in place against the outer legs. It's important to leave enough space between the two pairs of legs for easy movement when the legs are opened or closed. With the assembled table facedown on your worksurface, drill ¼-in.-dia. pilot holes through the pivot dowel (See Photo G). Cut the lock dowels to length, coat them with glue, and insert them.

FINISHING TOUCHES

⓳ Insert oak plugs with glue into the screw holes in the slats, let dry, and sand the plugged areas smooth. You could use wood filler instead of plugs, but the result will be less visually appealing.

⓴ Mask off painted surfaces of the table, and apply Danish oil or another clear exterior finish to the dowels and slats (See Photo H).

PHOTO G: Lock the inner legs in place by drilling and inserting ¼-in.-dia. dowels through the leg pivot dowel. Position the lock dowels to leave a slight bit of room between the legs, so they can move easily past one another without damaging the painted finish of the parts.

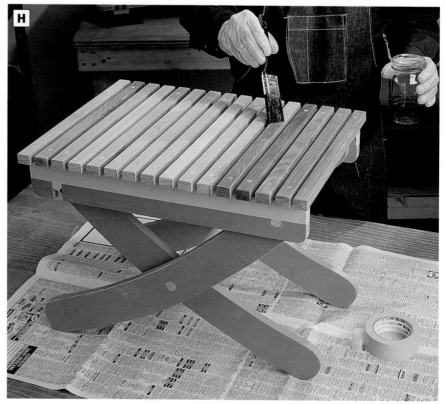

PHOTO H: Coat all raw wood, including the dowels, with Danish oil or another clear exterior-rated wood finish to protect the wood from UV rays and moisture exposure. Use masking tape to keep painted surfaces clean when you brush the slats and dowels with wood finish.

Porch Glider

The gentle rocking motion of this two-person porch
glider will make it one of your favorite summer spots.
Built entirely of solid red oak, this charming piece of furniture is destined to become a family heirloom. Set it in a
sheltered area, sit back and enjoy!

Vital Statistics: Porch Glider

TYPE: Porch glider

OVERALL SIZE: 27D by 59¾L by 35H

MATERIAL: Red oak

JOINERY: Butt joints reinforced with dowels or screws

CONSTRUCTION DETAILS:
- Many parts of the bench constructed with dowel joints for ease of construction and durability
- Bench suspended from stand by way of oak glider arms and pivoting hinges
- Screw heads concealed with matching oak plugs

FINISHING OPTIONS: Penetrating UV protectant sealer

Building time

PREPARING STOCK
1-2 hours

LAYOUT
3-4 hours

CUTTING PARTS
3-4 hours

ASSEMBLY
8-12 hours

FINISHING
2-4 hours

TOTAL: 17-26 hours

Tools you'll use

- Band saw
- Power miter saw or circular saw
- Table saw
- Drill press
- ⅜-in.-dia. plug cutter
- Drill/driver
- Drill bits (½-, 1-in.)
- Doweling jig
- Clamps
- Router with ¼-in. roundover bit
- Wooden mallet
- Flush-trimming saw
- Wrenches
- Combination square

Shopping list

- ☐ (1) 1½ × 8 in. × 4 ft. red oak
- ☐ (1) 1½ × 5½ in. × 4 ft. red oak
- ☐ (6) 1½ × 3½ in. × 8 ft. red oak
- ☐ (1) 1½ × 2½ in. × 4 ft. red oak
- ☐ (5) ¾ × 3 in. × 6 ft. red oak
- ☐ (2) ¾ × 2½ in. × 8 ft. red oak
- ☐ (1) ¾ × 1¾ in. × 6 ft. red oak
- ☐ (84) ⅜-in.-dia. × 2-in. fluted dowels
- ☐ Moisture-resistant wood glue
- ☐ Flathead wood screws (1½-, 2½-in.)
- ☐ (8) pivot hinges (available from Rockler Companies)
- ☐ UV protectant sealer

Porch Glider

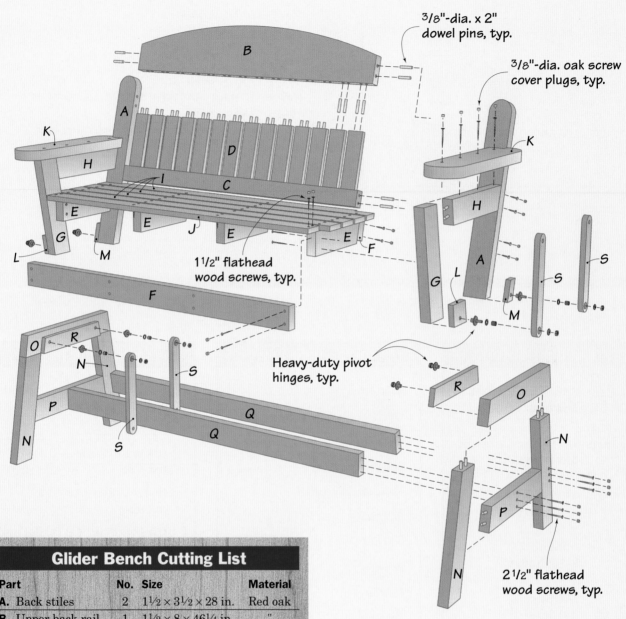

3/8"-dia. x 2" dowel pins, typ.

3/8"-dia. oak screw cover plugs, typ.

1 1/2" flathead wood screws, typ.

Heavy-duty pivot hinges, typ.

2 1/2" flathead wood screws, typ.

Glider Bench Cutting List

Part		No.	Size	Material
A.	Back stiles	2	$1\frac{1}{2} \times 3\frac{1}{2} \times 28$ in.	Red oak
B.	Upper back rail	1	$1\frac{1}{2} \times 8 \times 46\frac{1}{4}$ in.	"
C.	Lower back rail	1	$1\frac{1}{2} \times 2\frac{1}{2} \times 46\frac{1}{4}$ in.	"
D.	Back slats	14	$\frac{3}{4} \times 2\frac{1}{2} \times 8\frac{3}{4}$ in.	"
E.	Bench struts	4	$1\frac{1}{2} \times 3\frac{1}{2} \times 12\frac{1}{2}$ in.	"
F.	Bench rails	2	$1\frac{1}{2} \times 3\frac{1}{2} \times 50\frac{1}{4}$ in.	"
G.	Bench legs	2	$1\frac{1}{2} \times 3\frac{1}{2} \times 16\frac{3}{8}$ in.	"
H.	Arm supports	2	$1\frac{1}{2} \times 3\frac{1}{2} \times 15\frac{1}{2}$ in.	"
I.	Bench slats	4	$\frac{3}{4} \times 3 \times 53\frac{1}{4}$ in.	"
J.	Front bench slat	1	$\frac{3}{4} \times 3 \times 50\frac{1}{4}$ in.	"
K.	Arm rests	2	$1\frac{1}{2} \times 5\frac{1}{2} \times 23$ in.	"
L.	Bench leg blocking	2	$\frac{3}{4} \times 3 \times 4\frac{1}{16}$ in.	"
M.	Back stiles blocking	2	$\frac{3}{4} \times 3 \times 2\frac{3}{8}$ in.	"

Glider Stand Cutting List

Part		No.	Size	Material
N.	Stand legs	4	$1\frac{1}{2} \times 3\frac{1}{2} \times 18$ in.	Red oak
O.	End top rails	2	$1\frac{1}{2} \times 3\frac{1}{2} \times 21\frac{1}{4}$ in.	"
P.	End bottom rails	2	$1\frac{1}{2} \times 3\frac{1}{2} \times 18\frac{1}{16}$ in.	"
Q.	Stand stretchers	2	$1\frac{1}{2} \times 3\frac{1}{2} \times 58\frac{1}{2}$ in.	"
R.	Spacers	2	$\frac{3}{4} \times 2\frac{1}{2} \times 14\frac{1}{4}$ in.	"
S.	Glider arms	4	$\frac{3}{4} \times 1\frac{3}{4} \times 13\frac{1}{8}$ in.	"

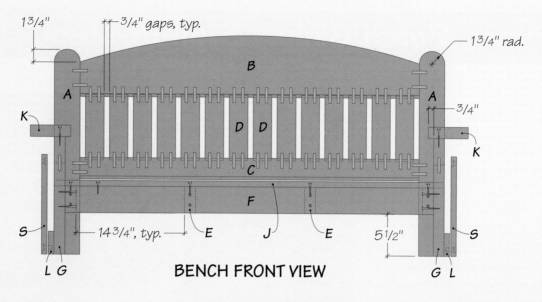

1 3/4"

3/4" gaps, typ.

B

1 3/4" rad.

A   A

K   3/4"

D D   K

C

F

S   J   S

14 3/4", typ.   E   E

5 1/2"

L G   G L

BENCH FRONT VIEW

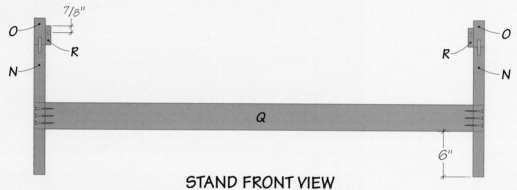

7/8"

O   O

R   R

N   N

Q

6"

STAND FRONT VIEW

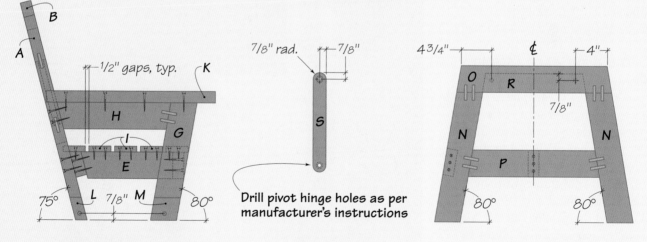

B

A

1/2" gaps, typ.   K

H

G

I

E

75°   L 7/8" M   80°

7/8" rad.   7/8"

S

Drill pivot hinge holes as per
manufacturer's instructions

4 3/4"   ¢   4"

O   R

7/8"

N   N

P

80°   80°

BENCH SIDE VIEW   **GLIDER ARMS**   **STAND SIDE VIEW**

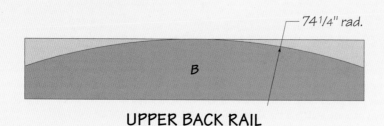

74 1/4" rad.

B

UPPER BACK RAIL

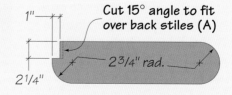

Cut 15° angle to fit
over back stiles (A)

1"

2 3/4" rad.

2 1/4"

ARM RESTS

This porch glider is made up of two distinct structures joined together with glider arms and pivot hinges. The hinges we used are available from the Rockler Companies. You'll start by building the bench, then the glider stand. After both parts are constructed, you'll join them together. All the face screws in this piece are countersunk 1/4 in. and concealed with 3/8-in.-dia. matching oak plugs. Building the glider will require you to make many angled cuts. Assembly will go much more smoothly if you take the time to make these angled cuts precisely.

BUILD THE BACK ASSEMBLY

❶ Make the upper and lower back rails. Cut workpieces for both parts to length from 1½-in.-thick stock. Mark the arched profile on the upper back rail, using the *Upper Back Rail* drawing, page 79, as a layout guide. Cut the profile on your band saw (**See Photo A**). Sand the profile smooth, and save the curved waste pieces to use later as clamping cauls.

❷ Drill dowel holes for the back slats in the upper and lower rails. Clamp the rails together, face to face, holding the ends and dowel edges flush. Mark centerlines for drilling the dowel holes by measuring 1½ in. from one end of the rails to the center of the first hole,

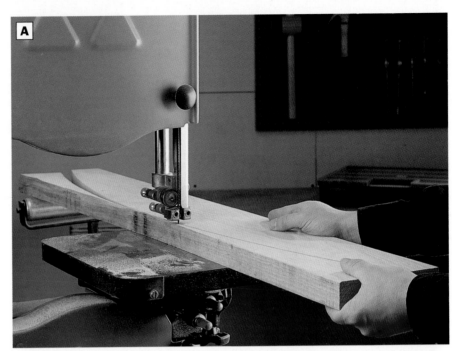

PHOTO A: Cut the profile on the upper back rail to shape on the band saw. Save the curved cutoff pieces to use as cauls when you clamp the back rails and slats together later.

Bench slat

PHOTO B: A right-angle jig will make the job of drilling dowel holes in the slats quicker and more precise. Tip the drill press table vertically and clamp the jig in place so the bit aligns with the dowel locations on each slat. Flip the slats edgewise and endwise to drill all four holes.

1 in. from that mark to the center of the second hole and 2¼ in. from the second mark to the third hole. From that point on, alternate 1-, and 2¼-in. spaces. The final measurement at the other end should be 1½ in. Unclamp the rails and drill the dowel holes, using a doweling jig as a guide. Each hole should be ⅝ in. deep, to allow clearspace at the bottom of the holes for glue.

❸ Make the back slats. Cut the 14 slats to length, then make a right-angle jig for your drill press to drill the dowel holes in the slat ends. The centerlines of the holes should be ¾ in. from each edge, leaving a 1-in. space between them. Tip your drill press table into the vertical position. Clamp the right-angle jig to the table with a slat in place, and adjust the jig position to achieve the correct hole position. Once the jig is set up, four dowel holes can be drilled in each back slat without changing the jig setting. Flip the slats edge-for-edge and end-for-end to drill the holes (**See Photo B**).

❹ Assemble the back rails and slats. Glue and insert two fluted dowels into one end of each of the back slats, then put a spot of glue in the holes in the lower back rail and on the mating surfaces of these joints. Tap the back slats into place against the rail with a wooden mallet. Insert glued dowels into the top ends of the slats, spread a thin layer of glue on the mating surfaces of the slats and the top back rail, and install this rail. Use the curved cutoffs from the upper rail as clamping cauls, and clamp up the back assembly (**See Photo C**).

❺ Make the back stiles. Cut the stiles to length, then bevel-cut the

PHOTO C: Assemble the upper and lower back rails and back slats with glue and dowels. Clamp the assembly together, using the waste pieces from Step 1 to make clamping the top rail easier. Alternate the clamps above and below the assembly to distribute clamping pressure evenly.

PHOTO D: Complete the back assembly by attaching the stiles to the back rails. Fasten the stiles to the ends of the rails with pairs of dowels and moisture-resistant wood glue.

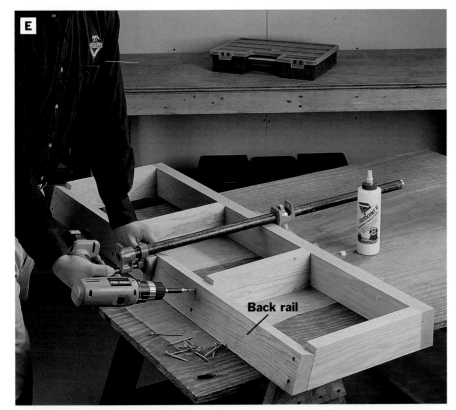

PHOTO E: Build the bench frame by installing four struts between the front and back bench rails with glue and screws. In this photo, the bench frame is upside down. Notice that the beveled edge of the back rail lines up with the edges of the struts, leaving an offset on the other edge.

PHOTO F: Fasten the back assembly to the bench frame by driving countersunk screws through the stiles and into the back bench rail. Be sure the bottom beveled ends of the stiles are parallel with the bottom edges of the bench.

bottom ends of the stiles to 15°, using a power miter saw. Mark the arcs on the upper ends of the stiles and cut them with a jig saw.

❻ Drill pairs of matching dowel holes in the stiles and rails to join the rails to the back assembly. On your worksurface, lay the stiles in position against the ends of the upper and lower rails. The top corners of the top back rail should be 1¾ in. down from the tops of the stiles. Mark the dowel hole locations and use a doweling jig as a guide to drill the ⅜-in.-dia. dowel holes, two dowels per joint.

❼ Attach the back stiles. Insert glued dowels into the holes, spread a thin coat of glue on the mating surfaces of the rails and stiles, and clamp the parts together (See Photo D). Protect the wood from clamp marks by using wooden cauls between the clamp jaws.

❽ Ease the outer edges of the back frame assembly with your router and a ¼-in. roundover bit.

BUILD & ATTACH THE BENCH FRAME

❾ Make the bench struts. Cut the struts to length. Then cut one end of each strut at a 75° angle across the width of the strut.

❿ Cut both bench rails to length, and rip one edge of the back bench rail at a 15° angle on the table saw (See *Bench Side View,* page 79).

⓫ Build the bench frame. Mark the locations of the struts on the inner faces of the bench rails—two flush with the ends of the rails and the other two struts spaced 14¾ in. from the end struts. The beveled edge of the back bench rail should be flush with the tops of the struts when the bench is right-side-up. Drill pairs of countersunk pilot holes in the rails, and fasten the rails to the struts with wood glue and 2½-in. flathead wood screws (**See Photo E**).

⓬ Attach the back assembly to the bench frame. When attached, the bottom edge of the bench frame is parallel to the angled cut at the bottom end of the stiles and 5½ in. above it. Clamp the back in position against the bench, drill countersunk pilot holes, and screw the stiles to the back rail (**See Photo F**).

Build & attach the arm assemblies

The arm assemblies consist of the bench legs and arm supports, joined together with dowels. When you attach the assemblies to the bench frame and back, be sure that the bottoms of the legs are even with the bottoms of the back stiles. Otherwise, the bench will not hang evenly later on when attached to the glider stand.

⓭ Cut the bench legs and arm supports to size, with their ends angled to 80°, as shown in the *Bench Side View* drawing, page 79.

⓮ Mark and drill dowel holes for connecting the arm supports and legs together. Lay out two dowels per joint. As before, butt the two mating parts together, draw a single line across the joint for each dowel, and drill straight holes for the dowels with a doweling jig (**See Photo G**).

⓯ Connect the arm supports and legs. Insert glued dowels into the holes and spread glue on the mating surfaces. Use wooden cauls to protect the finished surfaces of the parts, and join the arm supports to the legs with clamps.

PHOTO G: Join the bench legs to the arm supports with pairs of 2-in. fluted dowels. Use a doweling jig when you drill the holes to be sure that the dowel holes are drilled straight across the joints. Wrap a piece of tape around the drill bit to serve as a temporary depth stop.

PHOTO H: Fasten the arm assemblies to the bench by driving screws through the back stiles and into the arm supports. Screw from inside the bench to attach the end bench struts to the legs as well. Clamp the arm assemblies in place first, to make installing the assemblies easier.

PHOTO I: Cut the arm rests to shape, ease the edges with a router and roundover bit, then clamp them on top of the arm supports. Attach the rests to the supports with countersunk screws.

PHOTO J: Build the glider stand ends by attaching the top and bottom end rails to the stand legs with dowels and glue. The bottom rails fit between the legs, while the rop rails overlap the top ends of the legs.

16 Fasten the arm assemblies to the bench. Use a square to make a mark 5½ in. up from the bottom of both legs. Clamp the arm assemblies in position, so your leg marks align with the bottom edges of the bench frame, and the backs of the arm supports rest against the back stiles. Drill countersunk pilot holes through the back stiles into the arm supports, and fasten the stiles to the supports with 2½-in. screws. Then drill pilot holes and drive screws from inside the bench through the outer bench struts and into the bench legs (**See Photo H**).

COMPLETE THE BENCH

17 Cut and position the bench slats. Cut the bench slats and the front bench slat to length. Ease the edges and ends on the top face of each slat with a router and ¼-in. roundover bit. Lay the slats in place on the bench frame so the back edge of the front slat is even with the back edge of the legs. Allow for ½-in. spaces between the slats. Mark the rear slat so it will notch around the back stiles. Cut out the notches on this slat with your jig saw.

18 Fasten the slats to the bench struts. Use two screws per strut location on the slats, centering the screws on the thickness of the struts. Drill countersunk pilot holes and fasten the slats in place with 1½-in. flathead wood screws.

19 Cut and attach the arm rests. Refer to the *Arm Rests* drawing, page 79, to lay out the shape of the parts. Cut the arm rests to size and shape with radiused ends and notched back corners. NOTE: *The easiest way to determine the 15° notch angle is to simply set each arm rest in position on the arm supports and mark the angle where the* *arm rests cross the back stiles.* Ease all the arm rest edges except the notched portion with a router and a ¼-in. roundover bit. Clamp the arm rests in place, drill countersunk pilot holes, and fasten them to the arm supports with 2½-in. flathead wood screws (**See Photo I**).

❷⓪ Cut and attach the blocking pieces for the legs and stiles. Cut blanks to size for the four blocking pieces, hold them in place against the legs and stiles and mark the angle cuts. Cut the angles on a band saw. Apply an even coating of glue on the mating surfaces, clamp firmly and let dry completely. NOTE: *Since these parts are fastened with glue alone, it is important to build the best glue joints possible. Be sure the mating surfaces are flat and clean before gluing the joints.* Sand the edges flush and, if desired, ease the sharp edges with your router and a ¼-in. roundover bit.

BUILD THE STAND ENDS
❷① Cut out the stand legs, top and bottom rails. Refer to the *Stand Side View* drawing, page 79, for details on determining the angled ends of these parts.

❷② Drill pairs of dowel holes to attach the stand legs to the rails. Butt mating surfaces together, positioning the bottom rails 6 in. up from the bottoms of the legs. Mark the dowel locations and drill the holes with a doweling jig.

❷③ Assemble the stand ends. Insert glued dowels into the ends of the bottom rails, apply glue to the mating surfaces, and slide the legs into place over the dowels and against the bottom rails. Attach the top rails to the ends of the legs similarly. Clamp up the end assemblies (**See Photo J**).

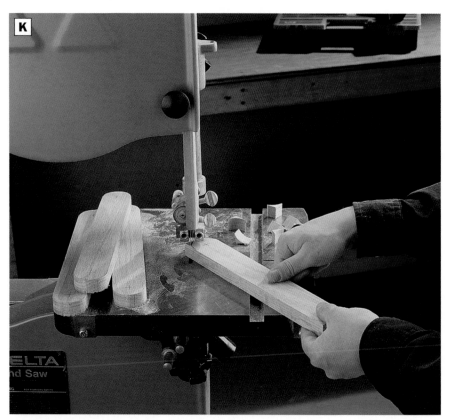
PHOTO K: Cut the four glider arms to shape on the band saw. Both ends of the arms receive ⅞-in.-radius curves. Sand the cut edges smooth and round them over with a router if you wish.

PHOTO L: Bore ⁵/₁₆-in.-deep, 1-in.-dia. counterbores on both ends of the glider arms. Notice that the counterbores are on opposite faces of the arms. Then drill a ½-in.-dia. hole through the center of the counterbores all the way through the arms, to accommodate the pivot hinges.

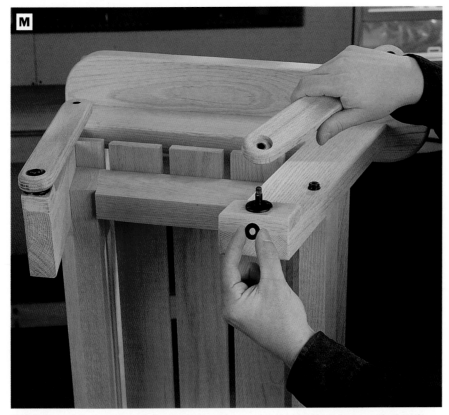

PHOTO M: Install pivot hinges to connect the glider arms to the blocking pieces on the bench. The hardware is essentially a shaft that slides inside a plastic bushing in the glider arms. The hinges press into holes in the blocking and hold the arms in place with washers and nuts.

PHOTO N: Set the bench on your worksurface so the glider arms hang freely. Attach the glider arms to the blocking pieces on the glider stand end assemblies with pivot hinges.

24 Install the spacers. Cut the spacers to size and shape, and fasten them to the inside faces of the end assembly top rails with glue. The bottom edges of the spacers should be flush with the bottom edges of the end top rails.

MAKE THE GLIDER ARMS

25 Cut four blanks for the glider arms to length and width. Mark the 7⁄8-in.-radius arc on the ends, and cut the arcs on your band saw **(See Photo K)**. Sand the cut edges smooth.

26 Drill the counterbored pivot hinge-mounting holes. Each of the hinge holes needs a 5⁄16-in.-deep by 1-in.-dia. counterbore to recess the pivot hinge washer and nut. Drill the 1-in. counterbores first, then drill 1⁄2-in.-dia. through holes at the center of the counterbores **(See Photo L)**. Note in the photo that the two holes in each arm are counterbored from opposite sides of the arms.

27 Attach the glider arms to the bench. Locate and drill the 1⁄2-in.-dia. × 1⁄2-in.-deep hinge holes in the blocking pieces at the ends of the bench. The holes should be centered across the width of the blocking pieces and 7⁄8 in. up from the bottom of the blocking. Install the lower pivot hinges and connect the glider arms to the bench, according to the manufacturer's instructions **(See Photo M)**.

INSTALL THE BENCH IN THE GLIDER STAND

28 Attach the stand end assemblies to the glider arms. Locate and drill the 1⁄2-in.-dia. × 1⁄2-in.-deep hinge holes in the spacers attached to the end top rails. The *Stand Side View* drawing, page 79, identifies the exact location of the hinges on the glider stand spacers. Support the bench structure on a platform so the stand ends can rotate freely, and install the upper pivot hinges and glider arms (**See Photo N**).

㉙ Install the stand stretchers. Cut the stretchers to length, and round over the edges. Mark the position of the stretchers on the glider stand ends—one stretcher is centered on the bottom rails, and the other stretcher lines up with the back edge of the back legs. Clamp the stretchers in place between the stand ends, and drive 2½-in. screws through counterbored pilot holes to attach the parts (**See Photo O**).

Finishing touches
㉚ Plug all the visible screw holes. Cut ⅜-in.-dia. oak plugs with a plug cutter mounted in your drill press. Spread glue on the plugs and tap them into the screw counterbores with a wooden mallet (**See Photo P**). Trim the plugs flush with the surrounding wood and sand smooth.

㉛ Sand the completed project thoroughly. Finish the glider with two coats of UV protectant sealer.

Shelter the glider

If you build this project from red oak, place the glider in an area sheltered from direct contact with moisture. Red oak, though durable, is not as weather-resistant as other woods. Should you desire to build the glider for an exposed location, use white oak, cedar, teak or Honduras mahogany instead. And be sure to use galvanized or stainless-steel screws as fasteners.

PHOTO O: Install stretchers between the end assemblies of the glider stand with 2½-in. countersunk flathead wood screws. Clamp the stand's ends to hold them stationary as you fasten the stretchers in place.

PHOTO P: Conceal all exposed screw heads with oak plugs. You could use oak dowel for making the plugs, but the preferred method is to cut the plugs from the face grain of a piece of oak stock. This way, the plugs will match the wood grain direction of the bench slats.

Planters

Deck plants provide a graceful transition from the distinctly indoor space of your home to the distinctly outdoor space of your yard. Attractive planters filled with flowers, herbs and shrubs can transform your deck into a cozy and inviting outdoor "room." These planters are designed to be used either as enclosures for potted plants or to be lined with landscape fabric and filled with dirt. We built these planters for a cedar deck; for best results, build yours from the same material as your deck.

Vital Statistics: Planters

TYPE: Deck and railing planters

OVERALL SIZE: Railing planter: 7¼W by 35¼L by 7¼H
Deck planter: 16W by 20½L by 15⅛H

MATERIAL: Cedar, exterior plywood

JOINERY: Butt joints reinforced with galvanized finish nails and screws

CONSTRUCTION DETAILS:
· Railing planter fits over standard 2 × 6 railing cap
· Recessed bottoms and weep holes improve air circulation and drainage on both planters

FINISHING OPTIONS: UV protectant sealer, exterior paint or leave unfinished to weather naturally to gray

Building time

PREPARING STOCK
0 hours

LAYOUT
1-2 hours

CUTTING PARTS
1-2 hours

ASSEMBLY
2-3 hours

FINISHING
1-2 hours

TOTAL: 5-9 hours

Tools you'll use

· Circular saw
· Jig saw
· Drill/driver
· Clamps
· Hammer
· Nailset

Shopping list

☐ (3) 1 × 8 in. × 8 ft. cedar
☐ (1) ¾ × 12 × 12 in. exterior plywood
☐ Galvanized deck screws (1¼-in.)
☐ Galvanized finish nails (2-in.)
☐ UV protectant sealer

Planters

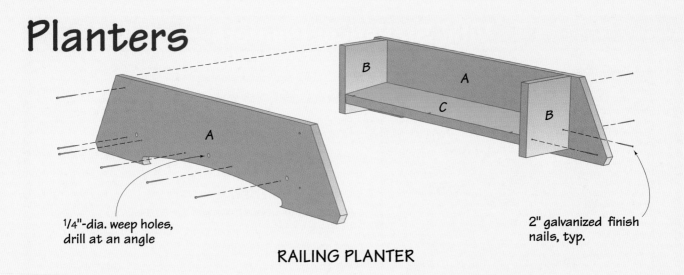

1/4"-dia. weep holes,
drill at an angle

2" galvanized finish
nails, typ.

RAILING PLANTER

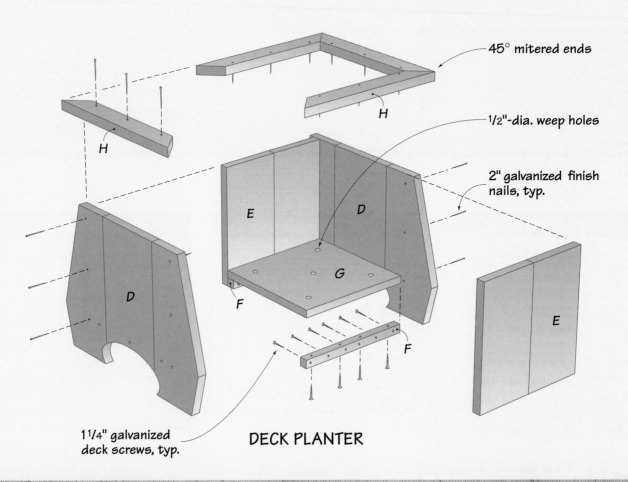

45° mitered ends

1/2"-dia. weep holes

2" galvanized finish
nails, typ.

1 1/4" galvanized
deck screws, typ.

DECK PLANTER

Planters Cutting List

Part	No.	Size	Material	Part	No.	Size	Material
Railing Planter				**Deck Planter**			
A. Sides	2	$\frac{7}{8}$ x $7\frac{1}{4}$ x $35\frac{1}{4}$ in.	Cedar	D. Sides	2	$\frac{7}{8} \times 20\frac{1}{2} \times 14\frac{1}{4}$ in.	Cedar
B. Ends	2	$\frac{7}{8}$ x $5\frac{1}{2}$ x $6\frac{1}{2}$ in.	"	E. Ends	2	$\frac{7}{8} \times 12 \times 12$ in.	"
C. Bottom	1	$\frac{7}{8}$ x $5\frac{7}{16}$ x 24 in.	"	F. Cleats	2	$\frac{7}{8} \times \frac{7}{8} \times 12$ in.	"
				G. Bottom	1	$\frac{3}{4} \times 12 \times 12$ in.	Exterior plywood
				H. Crown	4	$\frac{7}{8} \times 2 \times 16$ in.	Cedar

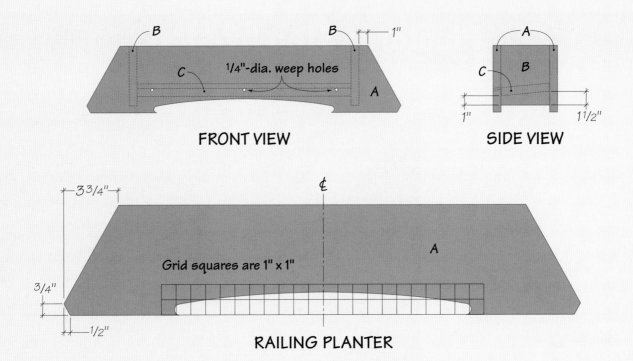

FRONT VIEW

B

B

1″

¼″-dia. weep holes

C

A

SIDE VIEW

A

C

B

1″

1½″

3¾″

¢

A

Grid squares are 1″ x 1″

3/4″

1/2″

RAILING PLANTER

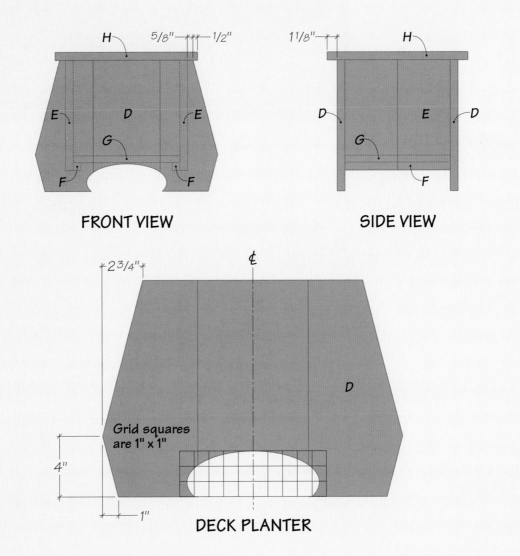

H

5/8″

1/2″

E

D

E

G

F

F

FRONT VIEW

1⅛″

H

D

E

D

G

F

SIDE VIEW

2¾″

¢

D

Grid squares
are 1″ x 1″

4″

1″

DECK PLANTER

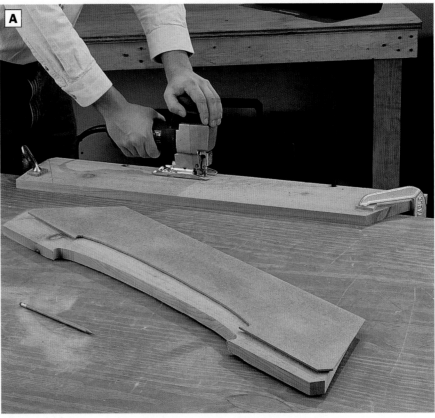

Cedar lumber is typically sold with one side rough and one side smooth. This feature provides you the opportunity to choose which surface to emphasize in the finished planters. For these planters, we held the rough side out because we wanted a casual, rustic look. If you prefer, you can achieve a more refined look simply by building your planters with the smooth surface out. If you intend to paint your finished planters, we recommend building with the smooth side out.

PHOTO A: Lay out and cut a template for making the sides of the railing planter, then use this template to draw the shapes on the side workpieces. Cut out the shapes with a jig saw.

RAILING PLANTER
CUT OUT THE PARTS

❶ Make a template for marking the two side profiles. Cut a piece of hardboard or stiff cardboard to size, 7¼ in. by 35¼ in., for use as a pattern. Following the *Railing Planter* drawing on page 91, mark the angles on the ends and the curved cutout profile on the bottom edge. Cut the template to shape with a jig saw and sand the cuts smooth.

❷ Trace the profile from the template onto the side workpieces.

❸ Cut out the sides. Clamp the blanks securely to your workbench and cut the profiles with your jig saw **(See Photo A)**.

❹ Cut the ends and bottom to

size, according to the dimensions in the *Cutting List* on page 90.

ASSEMBLE THE PLANTER

❺ Attach the ends to the bottom. The bottom is sloped to route seepage water away from your deck railing cap. Refer to the *Side View* drawing, page 91, and mark the slope of the bottom piece on the inside faces of the ends. Drill pilot holes in the ends. Clamp the bottom in place between the ends, and attach the parts with 2-in. galvanized finish nails **(See Photo B)**.

❻ Attach the sides. Lay the end/bottom assembly on your workbench. Center the first side piece on the assembly left-to-right

with all top edges flush. Clamp it in place. Note that the lower edges of the end pieces are ¾ in. above the lower edges of the sides; this allows the planter to rest on the railing cap while the sides overlap it for stability. Attach the side by driving galvanized finish nails through the side into the ends and the bottom. Use a nailset to recess the nailheads. Follow the same procedure to position and attach the remaining side.

❼ Drill the weep holes. Clamp the assembled planter to your worksurface with the deeper side of the compartment facing up. Drill three angled ¼-in.-dia. weep holes through the side of the planter into the deepest corner of

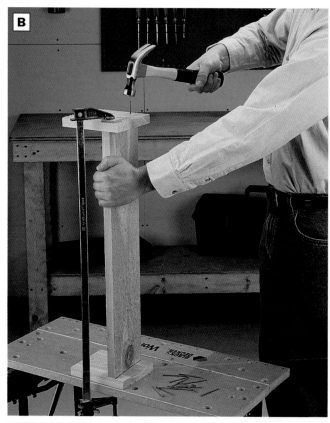

PHOTO B: Mark the slope of the bottom piece on the planter end pieces, then attach the ends to the bottom with galvanized finish nails. Clamp the pieces to help hold them steady during assembly.

PHOTO C: Fasten the planter sides to the ends and bottom with nails, then drill three angled ¼-in.-dia. weep holes through the side where the bottom of the planter slopes to its lowest point.

the compartment (**See Photo C**). Position the weep holes so they are just above the bottom piece inside the planter.

DECK PLANTER
MAKE THE SIDE PANELS

Each side panel is composed of three boards, which are held together during the construction process by a temporary cleat.

❶ Cut six pieces of 1 × 8 cedar to 14½ in. long (you'll need three pieces for each side).

❷ Cut two temporary cleats (not shown on the *Cutting List*) 13½ in. long from scrap wood.

❸ Build the sides. Lay groups of three boards facedown on your workbench in two groups. Center a temporary cleat left-to-right along the top edge of each group of

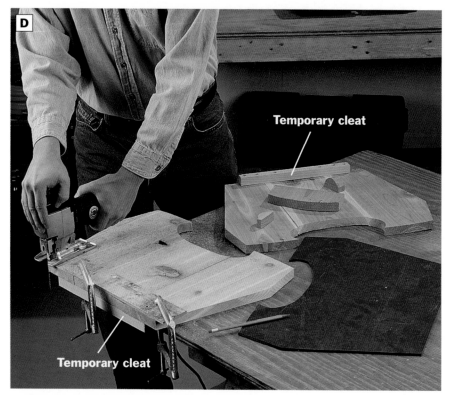

Temporary cleat

Temporary cleat

PHOTO D: Assemble two blanks for the deck planter sides using three lengths of 1 × 8 cedar per blank, fastened together with a temporary cleat. Mark the profiles on the side pieces with a template, then cut the sides to shape. You'll remove the temporary cleats later.

PHOTO E: Clamp pairs of 6-in.-wide boards for the end panels and fasten each panel together with a cleat. Use 1¼-in. galvanized screws to join the parts. These two cleats are permanent parts of the planter.

PHOTO F: Cut the bottom piece to size, drill five weep holes through the bottom for drainage, and fasten it to the cleats on the end pieces with countersunk screws. Attach the bottom so it will rest on the cleats when the planter is finished.

boards, and fasten each panel together by driving 1¼-in. wood screws through the cleat into the boards.

❹ Make a template for marking the profiles of the two sides. Cut a piece of hardboard or stiff cardboard 14¼ in. wide by 20½ in. long. Following the *Deck Planter* drawing on page 91, mark the angles on the ends and the shape of the curved cutout along the bottom edge. Cut the template to shape with a jig saw and sand the cut edges smooth.

❺ Trace the profile from the template onto the side panels. Draw on the face of the panels that does not have the cleats. Clamp each panel securely to your workbench and cut the parts with a jig saw (**See Photo D**).

MAKE THE ENDS & BOTTOM

The end panels are each composed of two boards fastened together with a permanent cleat.

❻ Rip a 4-ft., 1-in. length of 1 × 8 cedar to 6 in. wide. Cut the ripped board into four 12-in. lengths. Lay each pair of boards facedown on your workbench and clamp them together with the ends flush.

❼ Cut two pieces of scrap left over from Step 6 to ⅞ × ⅞ × 12 in. to form two cleats. Drill countersunk pilot holes in the cleats.

❽ Assemble the end panels by positioning a cleat flush with the bottom edges of each pair of boards and fastening the parts with 1¼-in. galvanized deck screws, screwing through the cleats into the end panels (**See Photo E**).

9 Cut the bottom to size from ¾-in. exterior plywood. Draw intersecting lines from corner to corner to use as a guide for locating and drilling five ½-in.-dia. weep holes.

ASSEMBLE THE PLANTER

10 Attach the end panels to the bottom. Clamp the bottom in place between the ends so it will rest on top of the cleats when the planter is right-side-up. Drill through the cleats from below to fasten the bottom (**See Photo F**).

11 Attach the sides. Position the first side panel on the end/bottom assembly so it is centered left-to-right and the top edges are all flush. Drive 2-in. galvanized finish nails through the side panel into the ends and the bottom, using a nailset to drive the nails below the surface of the wood. Attach the remaining side in the same fashion (**See Photo G**).

12 Unscrew and remove the temporary cleats from the side panels.

13 Cut the four crown pieces. Rip cedar stock to 2 in. wide. Measure your planter to verify the length of the crown pieces. The inside edges of the crown should sit flush with the inside of the planter when installed. Cut the pieces to length with the ends mitered at 45°.

14 Attach the crown pieces to the planter with finish nails (**See Photo H**).

FINISHING TOUCHES FOR BOTH PLANTERS

15 Break all edges with sandpaper and check that all nailheads are set. You may choose to leave the planters unfinished, apply the same finish as you have on your deck, or topcoat with paint.

PHOTO G: Fasten the sides to the end/bottom assembly by nailing through the sides and into the ends and bottom. Drill pilot holes before you drive the nails to keep the cedar from splitting. Once both sides are attached, remove the temporary cleats.

PHOTO H: Install the four crown pieces around the top of the planter with nails. Lay out and cut the crown pieces so they are mitered on the ends and fit flush with the inside of the planter.

Potting Bench

The gardeners in your family will wonder how they ever got along without this versatile potting bench. Ruggedly built to withstand hard use, this bench features a rolling cart for potting soil or compost, a drawer for all those small tools and the convenience of a ready water supply and sink. Whether you're mixing soil, repotting plants or rinsing vegetables, this attractive bench will make your gardening work more enjoyable and efficient.

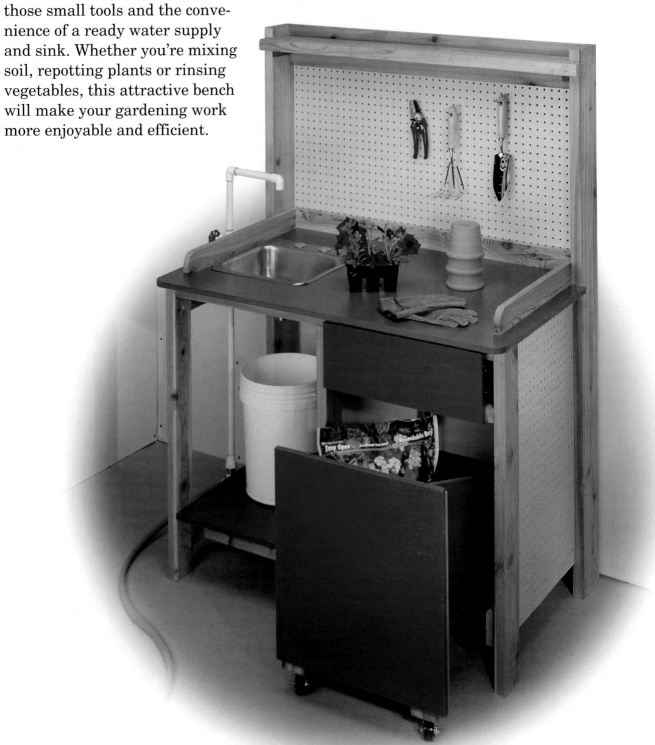

Vital Statistics: Potting Bench

TYPE: Potting bench

OVERALL SIZE: 48W by 28½D by 63½H

MATERIAL: Cedar, exterior plywood, perforated hardboard

JOINERY: Butt joints reinforced with galvanized deck screws

CONSTRUCTION DETAILS:

· Countertop outfitted with removable bar sink

· Shop-made PVC plumbing system designed for garden hose hook-up

· Cart outfitted with rolling casters

FINISHING OPTIONS: Cedar parts topcoated with penetrating UV protectant sealer, exterior paint or leave unfinished to weather naturally to gray. Hardboard and exterior plywood finished with exterior latex primer and paint

Building time

PREPARING STOCK
0 hours

LAYOUT
3-4 hours

CUTTING PARTS
2-3 hours

ASSEMBLY
5-8 hours

FINISHING
3-5 hours

TOTAL: 13-20 hours

Tools you'll use

· Circular saw

· Jig saw

· Drill/driver

· Clamps

· Combination square

· Hacksaw

Shopping list

Bench materials:

☐ (2) 2 × 6 in. × 6 ft. cedar
☐ (1) 2 × 6 in. × 4 ft. cedar
☐ (6) 2 × 4 in. × 8 ft. cedar
☐ (4) 2 × 2 in. × 8 ft. cedar
☐ (1) 1 × 6 in. × 4 ft. cedar
☐ (1) 1 × 3 in. × 8 ft. cedar
☐ (2) ¾ in. × 4 × 8 ft. exterior plywood
☐ (1) ¼ in. × 4 × 4 ft. perforated hardboard
☐ (4) 2-in.-dia. casters
☐ Galvanized deck screws (1¼-, 1½-, 2-, 2½-in.)
☐ Latex primer and paint
☐ UV protectant sealer

Plumbing parts:

☐ Stainless-steel bar sink
☐ ¾-in.-dia. PVC pipe (6 ft.)
☐ (2) strap clamps
☐ (2) 90° elbows
☐ PVC stop valve
☐ PVC female adaptor
☐ Hose thread to pipe thread transition fitting
☐ Angled hose fitting
☐ CPVC primer and cement

Potting Bench

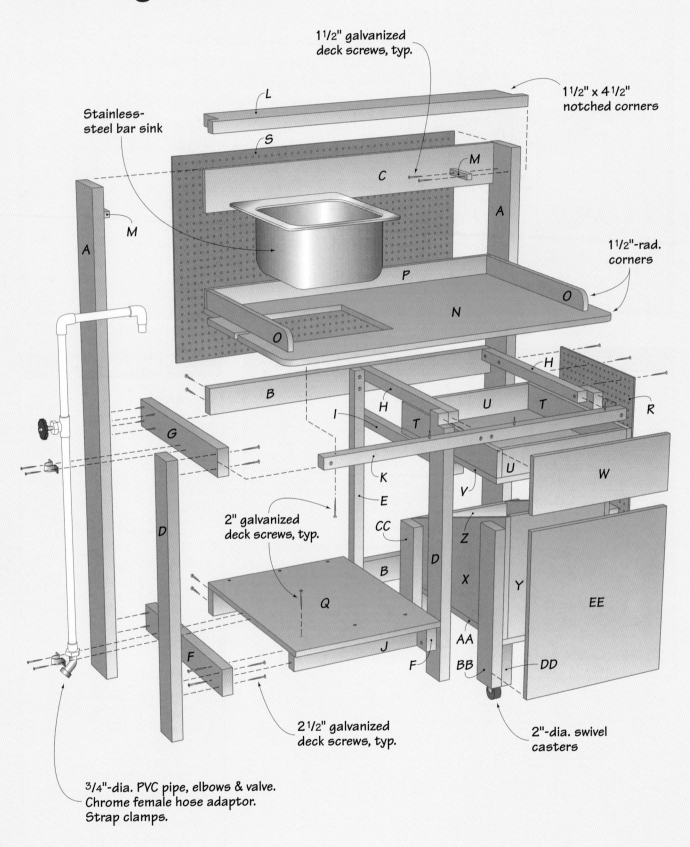

1½" galvanized deck screws, typ.

1½" x 4½" notched corners

Stainless-steel bar sink

1½"-rad. corners

2" galvanized deck screws, typ.

2½" galvanized deck screws, typ.

2"-dia. swivel casters

¾"-dia. PVC pipe, elbows & valve. Chrome female hose adaptor. Strap clamps.

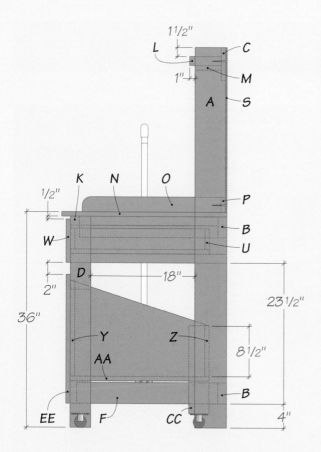

SIDE SECTION VIEW

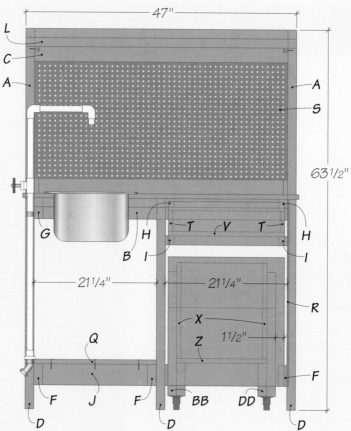

FRONT SECTION VIEW

Potting Bench Cutting List

Part	No.	Size	Material
A. Tall legs	2	$1\frac{1}{2} \times 5\frac{1}{2} \times 63\frac{1}{2}$ in.	Cedar
B. Back stretchers	2	$1\frac{1}{2} \times 3\frac{1}{2} \times 44$ in.	"
C. Shelf stretcher	1	$\frac{3}{4} \times 5\frac{1}{2} \times 44$ in.	"
D. Front legs	3	$1\frac{1}{2} \times 3\frac{1}{2} \times 35\frac{1}{4}$ in.	"
E. Rear support	1	$1\frac{1}{2} \times 1\frac{1}{2} \times 35\frac{1}{4}$ in.	"
F. Lower stretchers	3	$1\frac{1}{2} \times 3\frac{1}{2} \times 24\frac{1}{2}$ in.	"
G. Upper stretcher	1	$1\frac{1}{2} \times 3\frac{1}{2} \times 24$ in.	"
H. Drawer stretchers	2	$1\frac{1}{2} \times 1\frac{1}{2} \times 24$ in.	"
I. Drawer slides	2	$1\frac{1}{2} \times 1\frac{1}{2} \times 27$ in.	"
J. Bottom stretcher (Front)	1	$1\frac{1}{2} \times 3\frac{1}{2} \times 18\frac{1}{4}$ in.	"
K. Top stretcher (Front)	1	$1\frac{1}{2} \times 1\frac{1}{2} \times 44$ in.	"
L. Shelf	1	$1\frac{1}{2} \times 5\frac{1}{2} \times 47$ in.	"
M. Shelf cleats	2	$\frac{3}{4} \times \frac{3}{4} \times 4\frac{1}{2}$ in.	"
N. Countertop	1	$\frac{3}{4} \times 28\frac{1}{2} \times 48$ in.	Exterior plywood
O. Side splashes	2	$\frac{3}{4} \times 2\frac{1}{2} \times 24$ in.	Cedar
P. Back splash	1	$\frac{3}{4} \times 2\frac{1}{2} \times 44$ in.	"

Part	No.	Size	Material
Q. Lower shelf	1	$\frac{3}{4} \times 27 \times 21\frac{1}{4}$ in.	Exterior plywood
R. Side panel	1	$\frac{1}{4} \times 18 \times 31\frac{1}{4}$ in.	Perforated board
S. Back panel	1	$\frac{1}{4} \times 27\frac{1}{2} \times 44$ in.	"
T. Drawer sides	2	$\frac{3}{4} \times 3\frac{1}{2} \times 24$ in.	Exterior plywood
U. Drawer ends	2	$\frac{3}{4} \times 3\frac{1}{2} \times 18\frac{3}{4}$ in.	"
V. Drawer bottom	1	$\frac{3}{4} \times 20\frac{1}{4} \times 24$ in.	"
W. Drawer face	1	$\frac{3}{4} \times 7\frac{1}{4} \times 20\frac{1}{4}$ in.	"

Cart Cutting List

Part	No.	Size	Material
X. Sides	2	$\frac{3}{4} \times 16 \times 24$ in.	Exterior plywood
Y. Front	1	$\frac{3}{4} \times 14\frac{1}{4} \times 16$ in.	"
Z. Back	1	$\frac{3}{4} \times 14\frac{1}{4} \times 8\frac{1}{2}$ in.	"
AA. Bottom	1	$\frac{3}{4} \times 15\frac{3}{4} \times 24$ in.	"
BB. Front legs	2	$1\frac{1}{2} \times 3\frac{1}{2} \times 20\frac{3}{4}$ in.	Cedar
CC. Back legs	2	$1\frac{1}{2} \times 3\frac{1}{2} \times 14\frac{3}{4}$ in.	"
DD. Leg cleats	4	$1\frac{1}{2} \times 3\frac{1}{2} \times 5\frac{1}{2}$ in.	"
EE. Face	1	$\frac{3}{4} \times 20\frac{1}{4} \times 21\frac{1}{2}$ in.	Exterior plywood

PHOTO A: Build the right assembly by attaching a drawer stretcher, drawer slide and lower stretcher between a tall leg and front leg. Fasten the parts together with 2½-in. deck screws. Use a combination square to draw layout lines for the parts and to check the joints for square.

BUILD THE BENCH FRAME

❶ Cut the following cedar parts to size: tall legs, front legs, drawer stretchers, drawer slides, upper stretcher and lower stretchers. Label each part in pencil to make the pieces easy to identify.

❷ Build the left (plumbing) end assembly. As shown in the exploded drawing on page 98, the left end consists of a tall leg and a front leg joined by an upper stretcher and one of the lower stretchers. Install the upper stretcher flush with the top of the front leg, and inset it 1½ in. on both the front and back legs to allow space for the front top stretcher and the back stretcher. Install the lower stretcher 4 in. above the floor, and hold it in 1½ in. at the back and 1 in. at the front. Square up the assembly, drill countersunk pilot holes and fasten the parts with 2½-in. galvanized deck screws. When completed, the overall depth from the back edge of the tall leg to the front edge of the front leg should be 27 in.

❸ Build the right end assembly. The right end consists of a tall leg, front leg, drawer stretcher, drawer slide and lower stretcher. Install the drawer stretcher just as you did for the upper stretcher in Step 2. Install the lower stretcher 4 in.

PHOTO B: Assemble the bench framework by attaching the two back stretchers, shelf stretcher and top front stretcher to the end assemblies. The ends of the stretchers should butt against the inside faces of the front and back legs. See Step 4 for exact stretcher placement.

above the floor, holding it in 1½ in. at the back and 1 in. at the front. Install the drawer slide 4¾ in. below the bottom edge of the drawer stretcher and flush with the outside edges of the legs. Fasten the whole assembly together with deck screws driven into countersunk pilot holes (**See Photo A**).

❹ Connect the end assemblies with stretchers. Cut to size and attach the two back stretchers, shelf stretcher and the front top stretcher (**See Photo B**). When you install the shelf stretcher, inset it ¼ in. from the back edges of the tall legs to allow for the thickness of the back panel. Position the back stretchers 4 in. and 35¼ in. from the bottoms of the back legs.

❺ Build and install the middle support assembly. Cut the rear support, front bottom stretcher and remaining front leg to size. Cut a 1½ × 1½-in. notch in the top end of the front leg (**See Photo C**). Fasten the rear support, front leg, drawer stretcher, drawer slide and lower stretcher together with deck screws.

❻ Stand the support assembly you made in Step 5 in place, and position it by attaching the front bottom stretcher with deck screws (**See Photo D**). Complete the installation by screwing the support to the top front stretcher and both back stretchers.

❼ Build the benchtop. Cut the countertop to size (see *Cutting List,* page 99) from exterior plywood. Mark and cut a 1½-in.-radius arc on both front corners. Cut a 2 × 5½-in. notch on the back corners so the countertop fits around the tall legs and overhangs the bench by ½ in. on each end.

PHOTO C: Notch the top front corner of the center front leg so it will fit around the top front stretcher. Then combine this leg with the rear support, drawer stretcher, drawer slide and lower stretcher to form the middle support assembly.

PHOTO D: Install the front bottom stretcher 3 in. back from the front ends of the lower stretchers to position the middle support assembly. Fasten the bottom stretcher in place, then attach the middle support assembly to the top front stretcher and back stretchers.

PHOTO E: Center the sink so it will hang over the storage area on the left side of the bench. Lay out the sink opening using the template provided by the manufacturer, and cut out the sink opening.

PHOTO F: Install the back splash and side splash pieces on the countertop, then fasten the countertop to the bench framework by driving screws through the stretchers from below and into the countertop.

Mark and cut a clearance slot in the left edge of the top, 1¼ in. wide by 1½ in. deep, for the plumbing assembly.

8 Position the sink on the countertop so it is centered above the open storage area on the left half of the bench. Mark and cut out the sink opening (**See Photo E**).

9 Cut the lower shelf, side panel and back panel to size. Then prime and paint the countertop, lower shelf and the side and back panels.

10 Cut out and attach the shelf cleats and the shelf to the tall legs. Position the cleats 3 in. from the tops of the tall legs, drill countersunk pilot holes and attach the cleats with 1½-in. galvanized deck screws. Notch the ends of the shelf (See drawing, page 98) to fit around the tall legs. Install the shelf with screws driven through the shelf stretcher from the back.

PHOTO G: Fasten the perfboard side and back panels to the bench framework with 1½-in. galvanized deck screws. Be careful not to overdrive the screws when installing the perfboard.

11 Cut out and attach the back and side splashes to the countertop. Clamp the back splash in place between the notches at the back of the countertop, and inset it ¼ in. from the back edge of the countertop to allow for the back panel. Drill countersunk pilot holes up through the bottom of the countertop and into the bottom edge of the back splash, then fasten it to the countertop with 2-in. galvanized deck screws. Round the top front corner of each side splash. Clamp the splashes in place and attach with screws.

⑫ Install the lower shelf to the back and bottom front stretchers with 2-in. deck screws.

⑬ Attach the countertop assembly to the bench with 2-in. screws (**See Photo F**).

⑭ Install the perfboard back and side panels (**See Photo G**).

BUILD THE DRAWER & CART

⑮ Cut the drawer sides, ends, bottom and face to size from ¾-in. exterior plywood.

⑯ Cut the plywood cart parts to size. To cut the angle on the cart sides, mark a point on each back edge 8½ in. from the bottom corner. Draw lines from each of these marks to the upper front corners (**See Photo H**). Cut the angles.

⑰ Prime all surfaces of the drawer and cart parts. Sand the surfaces and edges smooth first.

⑱ Assemble the drawer box. Apply glue to the ends of the end pieces, clamp the ends in place between the side pieces and assemble with 1½-in. galvanized deck screws (**See Photo I**). Position the drawer bottom, using it to square up the rest of the drawer structure. Fasten the bottom to the ends and sides with screws.

⑲ Assemble the cart box. As with the drawer, the ends are fastened between the sides, and the bottom piece fastens to the bottom edges of the ends and sides. Use counter-

PHOTO H: Cut the cart's angled sides by measuring 8½ in. along one short edge of each side panel. Connect this point to the top corner on the opposite edge with a straightedge. Cut these parts to shape. Assemble the sides, ends and bottom panel to form the cart box.

PHOTO I: Glue and screw the drawer ends to the side pieces, driving the screws through countersunk pilot holes to keep the plywood from splitting. Then, fasten the drawer bottom to the bottom edges of this drawer frame. Use the bottom as a guide for squaring up the drawer.

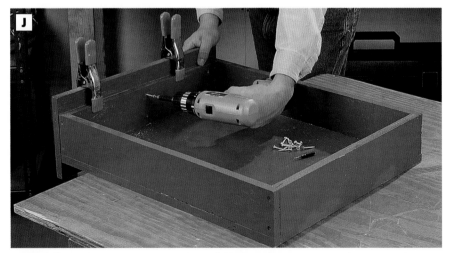

PHOTO J: Clamp the drawer face to the front of the drawer box so the ends of the drawer face are flush with the drawer sides. The face should overhang the top and bottom of the drawer by 1½ in. Fasten the drawer face with 1¼-in. deck screws, driven from inside the drawer.

PHOTO K: Install the leg assemblies to the cart box with 1½-in. screws. The front legs should butt against the back of the cart face. Attach the rear legs so they are flush with the cart back.

PHOTO L: Attach casters to the cart leg and cleat assemblies. We used swiveling locking casters on the front legs and fixed casters on the back. If you plan to fill the cart with dirt, be sure the casters are sturdy.

sunk 1½-in. screws for attaching the parts.

20 Paint the assembled drawer box and the loose drawer face, as well as the cart and the cart face. Apply two coats of exterior latex paint.

21 Attach the drawer face. Center the face on the front of the drawer box, flush on the ends and over-hanging 1½ in. on both the top and the bottom edges. Clamp the face in position, drill countersunk pilot holes and attach the face from inside the drawer with 1¼-in. galvanized deck screws **(See Photo J)**.

22 Attach the cart face. Note that the face is not centered on the cart: it overhangs 1½ in. on the left side, 3 in. on the right side and ½ in. at the top. Hold the face in position with spring clamps, and screw the face to the cart from inside the cart box.

23 Attach the cart legs and cart leg cleats. Cut the cart legs and cleats to size. Fasten the cleats to the legs with 2½-in. deck screws. Attach the legs to the cart with 2-in. deck screws **(See Photo K)**.

24 Attach the casters to the legs and cleats **(See**

Photo L). We used locking casters in the front so the cart stays in its place until you want to move it.

ADD THE PLUMBING

The sink is simply set loose into the countertop cut-out. It can drain either directly into a 5-gallon pail, or you can use a hose clamp to attach a length of flexible tubing to the drain tail and route it to your desired location. The "faucet" is fabricated from PVC and metal parts (See *Plumbing Parts*, next page) that are available from any local building supply center.

25 Fabricate the PVC water supply and faucet assembly. Cut the three sections of straight piping to length with a hacksaw. De-burr the cuts with a utility knife or emery paper. Dry-fit the PVC assembly together to make sure the lengths are correct. Draw an alignment mark across the fitting and pipe at every joint with a permanent marker to help you make the proper alignments quickly, once the pieces are cemented together. Disassemble the pieces.

26 Build the plumbing assembly. Prepare the joint surfaces by scuffing with emery cloth. When you make the joints, wear gloves and be sure your work

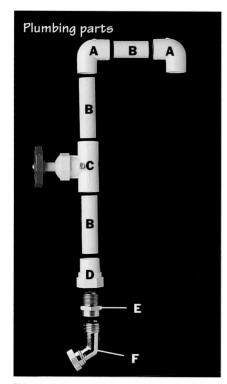

Plumbing parts

This plumbing system is designed to hook up to a garden hose for a water supply. To build it, you'll need: (A) 90° elbow; (B) ¾-in. PVC pipe; (C) PVC stop valve; (D) Female adaptor; (E) Hose thread to pipe thread transition fitting; (F) Angled hose connector.

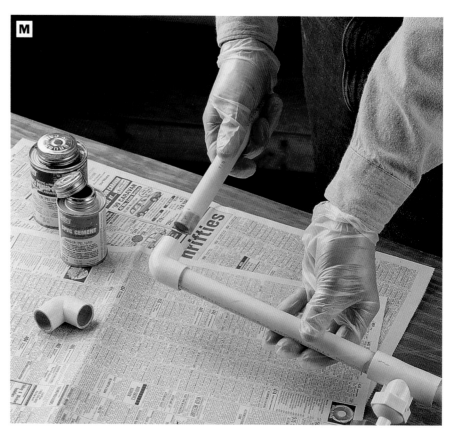

PHOTO M: Cut the straight pipe sections to length and dry-assemble the entire plumbing unit to check its fit on the potting bench. Then disassemble the PVC, prime the mating parts of each joint, and bond the PVC together with CPVC cement. Wear gloves when bonding the parts.

area is well ventilated. Make one joint at a time. Apply an even coat of PVC primer to both joint surfaces. Spread PVC cement onto the primed surfaces, following the directions on the can. Quickly slip the fitting and pipe together. Rotate the pieces a quarter turn to spread the glue evenly, and hold the parts in place with the marks aligned for approximately one minute (**See Photo M**).

㉗ Attach the plumbing assembly to the bench. Position the assembly in the countertop notch, and secure the plumbing with strap clamps (**See Photo N**).

FINISHING TOUCHES
㉘ Seal or paint the cedar parts of your bench as you like. No finish is actually required, but the cedar will turn gray if it isn't covered with a UV sealer.

PHOTO N: Use strap clamps to attach the plumbing assembly to the bench.

Art Deco
Hammock Stand

Are you among the many people who would love to while away a summer afternoon nestled in the comfort of a hammock, but you just don't have two conveniently spaced trees? Well, despair no more! This solid hammock stand goes where you want it to—your deck, porch, yard or poolside. The angled uprights and feet are conveniently friction-fit to allow for quick disassembly and easy off-season storage.

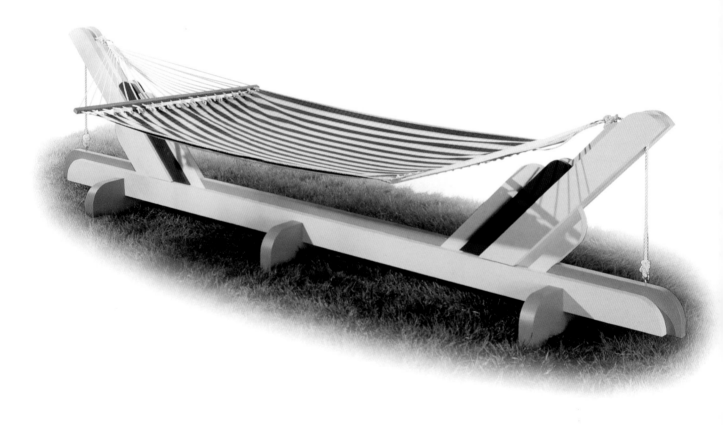

Vital Statistics: Art Deco Hammock Stand

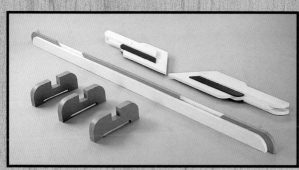

TYPE: Hammock stand

OVERALL SIZE: 24W by 14 ft. 5 in.L by 49H

MATERIAL: Pine

JOINERY: Butt joints reinforced with galvanized screws

CONSTRUCTION DETAILS:

· Legs notched to fit around base

· Uprights install like tenons into "mortise" spaces in base

· Supports and legs designed to be removable for seasonal storage (See bottom left photo)

FINISHING OPTIONS: Exterior latex primer and paint

Building time

PREPARING STOCK
0 hours

LAYOUT
2-3 hours

CUTTING PARTS
2-3 hours

ASSEMBLY
2-4 hours

FINISHING
3-5 hours

TOTAL: 9-15 hours

Tools you'll use

· Circular saw or power miter saw

· Compass

· Jig saw

· Drill/driver

· Clamps

· Combination square

· Belt sander

· Wood rasp or coarse wood file

Shopping list

☐ (2) 2 × 10 in. × 6 ft. pine

☐ (2) 2 × 8 in. × 6 ft. pine

☐ (2) 2 × 6 in. × 14 ft. pine

☐ (4) 2 × 6 in. × 8 ft. pine

☐ (2) 2 × 6 in. × 6 ft. pine

☐ (2) 1 × 4 in. × 6 ft. pine

☐ (2) 4-in. lag screw hooks

☐ Galvanized deck screws (1½-, 2½-in.)

☐ Latex primer

☐ Exterior latex paint

Art Deco Hammock Stand

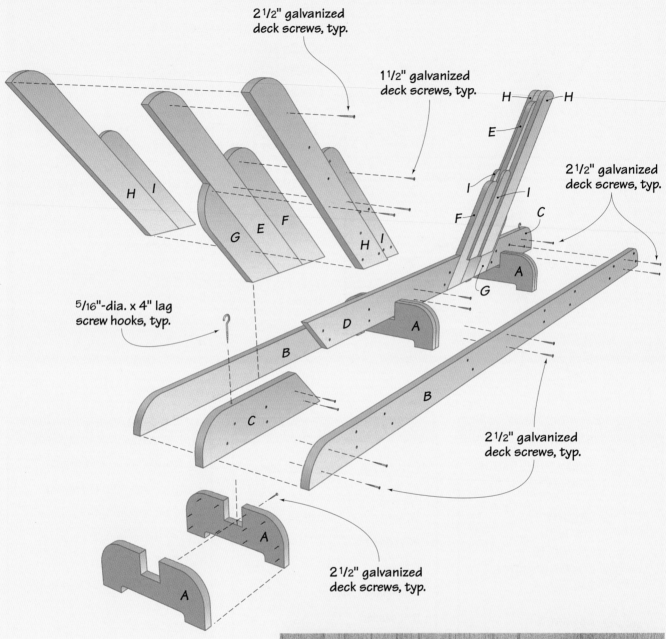

2¹/₂" galvanized deck screws, typ.

1¹/₂" galvanized deck screws, typ.

2¹/₂" galvanized deck screws, typ.

⁵/₁₆"-dia. x 4" lag screw hooks, typ.

2¹/₂" galvanized deck screws, typ.

2¹/₂" galvanized deck screws, typ.

Art Deco Hammock Stand Cutting List

Part	No.	Size	Material
A. Leg sections	6	1½ × 9¼ × 24 in.	Pine
B. Outer base	2	1½ × 5½ × 158 in.	"
C. Base ends	2	1½ × 7¼ × 31½ in.	"
D. Inner base	1	1½ × 7¼ × 68 in.	"
E. Center support	2	1½ × 5½ × 61 in.	"
F. Upper support brace	2	1½ × 5½ × 36 in.	"
G. Lower support brace	2	1½ × 5½ × 26 in.	"
H. Outer supports	4	1½ × 5½ × 57 in.	"
I. Support trim	4	¾ × 3½ × 30 in.	"

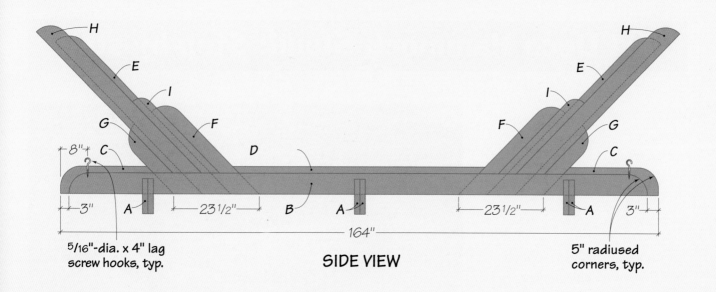

H
E
I
G
C
F
D
8"
3"
A
23 1/2"
B
A
23 1/2"
A
3"
164"
F
I
E
G
H
C
5/16"-dia. x 4" lag screw hooks, typ.

SIDE VIEW

5" radiused corners, typ.

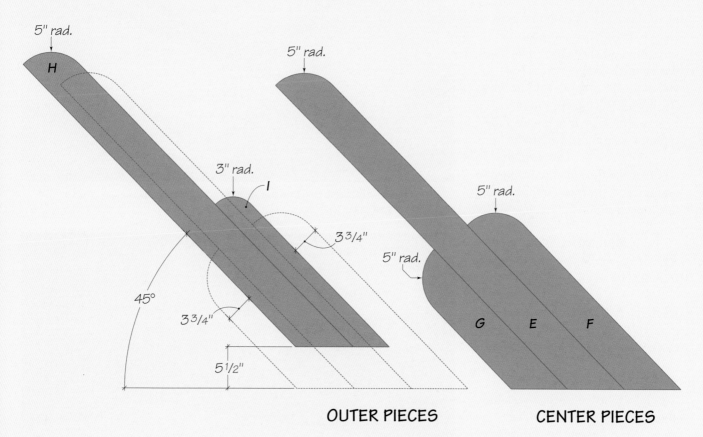

5" rad.
H

5" rad.

3" rad.
I

3 3/4"

45°

3 3/4"

5 1/2"

OUTER PIECES

5" rad.

5" rad.

G   E   F

CENTER PIECES

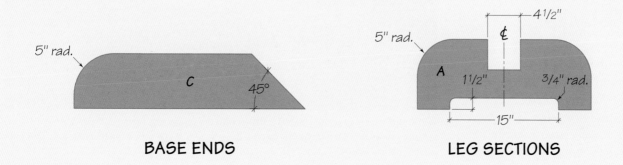

5" rad.
C
45°

BASE ENDS

5" rad.

4 1/2"
¢
A
1 1/2"
3/4" rad.
15"

LEG SECTIONS

Built completely from standard dimension pine lumber, this unique hammock stand is made up of three subassemblies—one center support, two angled uprights and three legs. The foundation of the project is its base, which forms a "sandwich" around the uprights. Gaps in the inner layer of the base function as mortises for holding the angled uprights in place. The uprights and feet are designed to fit into and around the base without the need for mechanical fasteners.

BUILD THE LEGS

❶ Cut the six leg blanks to length from 2 × 10 stock.

❷ Refer to the *Leg Sections* drawing, page 109, to draw leg profiles on the leg blanks (**See Photo A**).

❸ Fasten pairs of leg blanks together. Apply moisture-resistant glue between each pair of leg blanks, and fasten the workpieces with countersunk 2½-in. galvanized deck screws (**See Photo B**). Be sure to keep the screws clear of your layout lines.

❹ Cut the three legs to shape. Use a band saw or a jig saw and long wood-cutting blade to cut the leg profiles. NOTE: *If you prefer, you could also cut each of the six leg pieces to shape before fastening*

PHOTO A: Cut six leg blanks to size. Then use a compass and combination square to lay out the shapes of the legs on the leg blanks.

PHOTO B: Fasten pairs of leg blanks together with the layout side facing out. Use glue and countersunk screws to attach the parts. Cut the three legs to shape with a band saw or a jig saw, and smooth the cut edges.

them into pairs, but the parts will match more closely if they are cut together. Be careful not to cut the notch for the base too wide. The completed hammock stand will be much sturdier if the base fits snugly into the legs, and you can widen the notch slightly, if necessary, when test-fitting the components later before final painting.

⑤ Fill the leg screw holes with wood putty or auto body filler. Sand the surfaces and ease the edges, then coat the legs with latex primer.

BUILD THE BASE

⑥ Cut the two outer base pieces, base ends and the inner base to length. Scribe radiused corners on the outer base and base end pieces with a compass. Then mark the 45° angled ends on the base ends and the inner base. Cut the pieces to shape.

⑦ Paint the base parts with latex primer. Priming the parts now, while they are still separate and accessible, provides the best weather protection. Sand the surfaces and edges well before applying the primer.

⑧ Fasten the inner base to the one outer base piece with screws. Center the inner base on the outer base, with the bottom edges flush. For now, tack the inner base in place by driving two screws through it and into the outer base.

⑨ Attach the base ends. NOTE: *The hammock stand uprights will friction-fit between the inner base and the base ends, "mortise" style. To guarantee enough room for the uprights, lay three scrap pieces of 2 × 6 edge-to-edge on the ends of the inner base. Leave an additional ¼-in. space to allow for ease in inserting and removing the angled*

PHOTO C: Fasten the inner base and base ends to one outer base. Center the inner base on the outer base. Be sure to leave enough room between the inner base and base ends for the uprights. Use spacers and add ¼ in. Attach the parts with 2½-in. galvanized deck screws.

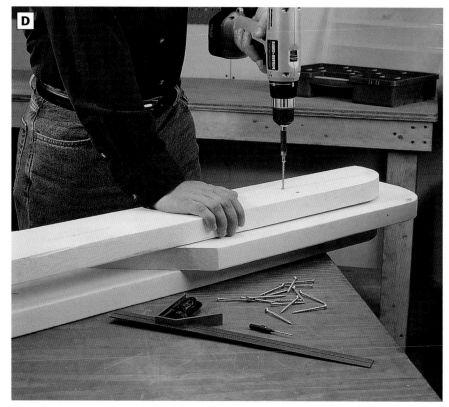

PHOTO D: Lay the other outer base piece on top of the base assembly and drive screws through it to attach it to the inner base pieces. Countersink pilot holes for the screws so you can conceal them with wood putty or auto body filler.

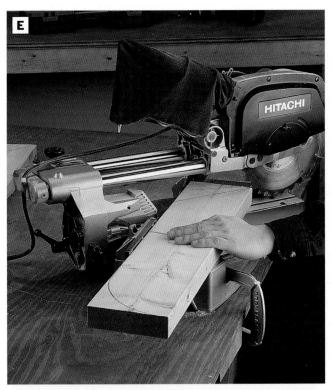

PHOTO E: Lay out and cut parts for the uprights. Each piece is angled to 45° on one end and has a radiused corner on the other end. A power miter saw will cut the angled ends accurately and quickly.

PHOTO F: Prime the parts for the uprights, and use a scrap 2 × 6 as a spacer to offset the outer upright parts from the center three support pieces. Drive screws through the outer pieces to build each upright.

uprights. With this spacing determined, fasten both base ends to the outer base with 2½-in. galvanized deck screws. Remove the 2 × 6 spacers.

⑩ Complete the attachment of the inner base by driving in the remaining screws (**See Photo C**).

⑪ Install the other outer base piece. Lay the outer base in position over the base ends and inner base, with the bottom edges flush. Drill countersunk pilot holes and attach the outer base with 2½-in. galvanized deck screws (**See Photo D**).

⑫ Fill screw holes in the outer base pieces, sand the surfaces smooth and spot-prime the screw locations.

BUILD THE ANGLED UPRIGHTS

⑬ Cut the center supports, upper and lower support braces, outer supports and the support trim pieces to size and shape. First cut the various blanks to length, as specified in the *Cutting List,* page 108. Mark the radiused corners on the support trim pieces with a compass. All these pieces have one corner cut at either a 5-in. or a 3-in. radius, and the other end cut at a 45° angle. Cut the angled ends with a power miter saw, circular saw or on a radial-arm saw (**See Photo E**). Then cut the curved profiles with a jig saw.

⑭ Prime the parts for the uprights. Be sure to sand the curved ends and ease sharp or rough edges before priming. Prime all part surfaces.

⑮ Assemble the uprights. On your worksurface, lay one center support between an upper and a lower support brace, as shown in the *Center Pieces* diagram, page 109. Clamp a scrap 2 × 6 board across the supports so that its lower edge is flush with the angled ends of the parts. Position the outer support and the support trim on top of the center support assembly, with their bottom angled ends tight against the top of the clamped 2 × 6. Drill countersunk pilot holes and attach the outer pieces to the center, upper and lower supports with galvanized deck screws (**See Photo F**). Stagger the screws so the outer pieces lock the three inner supports together. Unclamp the partially assembled upright, turn it over, and complete the assembly by positioning and attaching the other outer support and trim piece. Again, use the 2 × 6 as a spacer. Follow the same steps to build the second angled upright.

FINISHING TOUCHES

⑯ Before final painting, test-fit the uprights in the base. If the leg notches are too snug to fit around the base, enlarge them slightly with a wood rasp or a coarse file. The angled uprights may also need to be sanded slightly to slide easily into their mortises in the base, and the fit will get tighter once the wood is covered with paint. A belt sander will make quick work of this task. Sand the bottoms of the uprights just until the uprights slide easily into the base.

17 Fill remaining screw holes, and spot-prime any raw wood or wood filler, especially those areas you sanded in Step 16. Topcoat the base and angled supports with exterior latex enamel paint, using masking tape to protect adjoining areas of contrasting color (**See Photo G**). As you can see, we used a color scheme of grays and blues, to give the hammock stand a "silver streak" look. But you can easily substitute colors of your choice to suit your taste or to complement other outdoor furniture.

18 Install the 4-in. lag screw hooks 8 in. from each end of the base. Drill ¼-in.-dia. pilot holes for the hooks. It may help to wedge a wrench or a screwdriver in the curved portion of the hook and use it as a lever to twist the hooks into the base.

19 Hang the hammock. Assemble the uprights into the base. Install the hammock by stretching it from hook to hook with the rope running between the outer supports on the angled uprights (**See Photo H**). The end ropes should be short enough so that the hammock hangs taut without weight. NOTE: *You'll probably need to adjust and retighten the hammock ropes as the hammock and ropes stretch from use.*

PHOTO G: Mask off those hammock parts that you want to paint in contrasting colors. Use wide tape and "burnish" the edges of the tape with your fingernail where paint colors meet to keep one color from bleeding into the other as you paint. Paint one color at a time and allow it to dry.

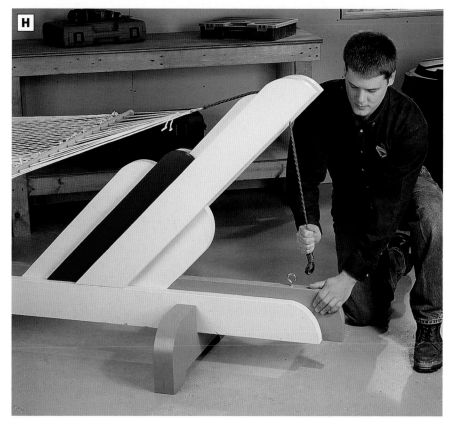

PHOTO H: Hang the hammock. Stretch the hammock ropes over the center support on each upright and pull the hammock until taut. Tie off the hammock securely to the lag screw hooks.

Sun Lounger

You'll find this handsome lounge chair perfect for relaxing outdoors, whether your preference is lying in the sun and working on your tan or enjoying shady summer breezes with the company of a good book. The back adjusts to four positions, so you're sure to be able to find the one that suits your mood and activity. The foot section also is adjustable for even greater versatility and comfort.

Vital Statistics: Sun Lounger

TYPE: Lounge chair

OVERALL SIZE: 24W by 80¾L by 14½H (38H with the back raised)

MATERIAL: Cedar, hardwood dowel

JOINERY: Butt joints reinforced with galvanized deck screws, stainless-steel bolts, washers and nuts

CONSTRUCTION DETAILS:
· Back rest adjusts to four positions by means of a pivoting back brace
· Foot rest is adjustable or removable

FINISHING OPTIONS: Penetrating UV protectant sealer, exterior paint or leave unfinished to weather naturally to gray

Building time

PREPARING STOCK
0 hours

LAYOUT
2-3 hours

CUTTING PARTS
3-4 hours

ASSEMBLY
3-5 hours

FINISHING
2-3 hours

TOTAL: 10-15 hours

Tools you'll use

· Circular saw, power miter saw or radial-arm saw

· Router with ½-in. roundover bit, ¾-in. core box bit

· Jig saw

· Drill/driver

· Clamps

· Sockets

· Combination square

· Bevel gauge

Shopping list

☐ (11) 2 × 4 in. × 8 ft. cedar

☐ (2) 1-in.-dia. × 3-ft. hardwood dowels

☐ (1) ¾-in.-dia. × 3-ft. hardwood dowels

☐ (4) ⅜ × 3½-in. stainless-steel bolts (12 washers, 8 nuts)

☐ Galvanized deck screws (2½-, 3-in.)

☐ Galvanized nails (#6d, #4d)

☐ UV protectant sealer

Sun Lounger

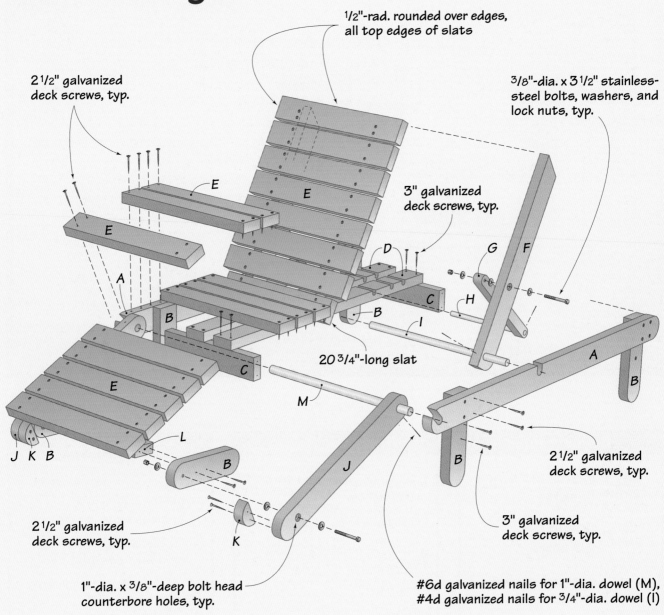

1/2"-rad. rounded over edges, all top edges of slats

2 1/2" galvanized deck screws, typ.

3/8"-dia. x 3 1/2" stainless-steel bolts, washers, and lock nuts, typ.

3" galvanized deck screws, typ.

20 3/4"-long slat

2 1/2" galvanized deck screws, typ.

3" galvanized deck screws, typ.

1"-dia. x 3/8"-deep bolt head counterbore holes, typ.

#6d galvanized nails for 1"-dia. dowel (M), #4d galvanized nails for 3/4"-dia. dowel (I)

Sun Lounger Cutting List

Part	No.	Size	Material	Part	No.	Size	Material
A. Seat rails	2	1½ × 3½ × 56¼ in.	Cedar	H. Adjustment dowel	1	¾ in. dia. × 18¾ in.	Hardwood
B. Legs	6	1½ × 3½ × 13 in.	"	I. Back rest dowel	1	1 in. dia. × 24½ in.	"
C. Seat stretchers	2	1½ × 3½ × 18 in.	"	J. Foot rest rails	2	1½ × 3½ × 27½ in.	Cedar
D. Back supports	2	1½ × 3½ × 46 in.	"	K. Leg stops	2	1½ × 3½ × 1¾ in.	"
E. Slats	19	1½ × 3½ × 24 in.	"	L. Foot rest stretcher	1	1½ × 3½ × 14⅞ in.	"
F. Back rails	2	1½ × 3½ × 31 in.	"	M. Foot rest dowel	1	1 in. dia. × 24½ in.	Hardwood
G. Adjustment braces	2	1½ × 1½ × 16½ in.	"				

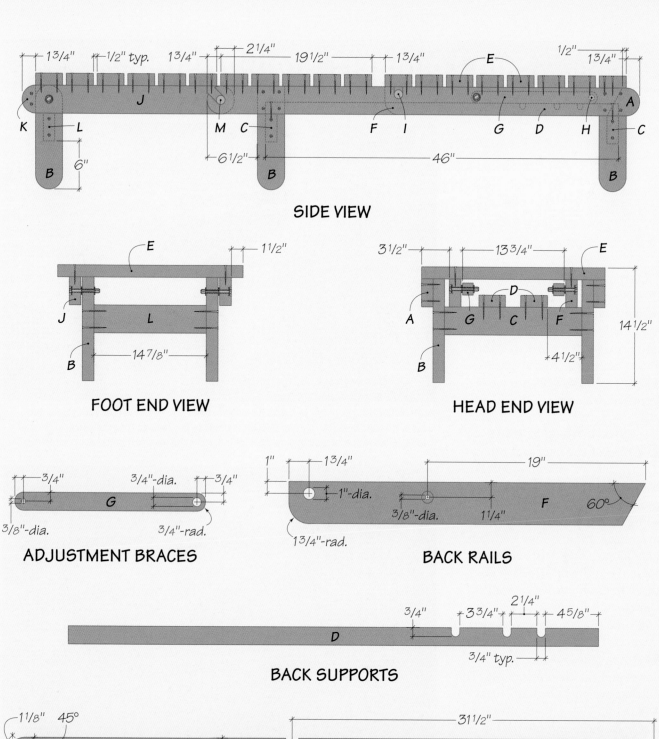

SIDE VIEW

FOOT END VIEW

HEAD END VIEW

ADJUSTMENT BRACES

BACK RAILS

BACK SUPPORTS

SEAT RAILS

FOOT REST RAILS

FOOT REST LEGS

The lounge chair is made up of three sections: a stationary seat, an adjustable back rest and an adjustable foot rest. The seat section provides the basic structure and is built first. All the parts, except for the dowels, are made from cedar 2 × 4s.

SHAPE THE SEAT RAILS

❶ Crosscut the long seat rails to length. Draw a 1¾-in. radius on both ends of each rail. Find the centerpoint of each radius by using a combination square and marking a 45° line from both corners at each end. Position your compass at the intersection of these lines and draw the radius. Cut out the curves with a jig saw, and sand the cut edges smooth.

❷ Cut notches for the foot rest dowel and the back rest dowel. The notches are made by first boring 1⅛-in.-dia. holes, then cutting a slot from these holes to the top edge of each rail. Start with the foot rest dowel notches. Using the centerpoint you established on the ends of the rails in Step 1, bore a 1⅛-in.-dia. hole. Draw two 45° lines to connect the hole to the top corner of the rails. Cut along these lines to form the foot rest notches **(See Photo A)**. Form the back rest notches by measuring 31½ in. from the ends of the rails opposite the foot rest notches. The center-

PHOTO A: Cut notches in the seat rails for back rest and foot rest dowels by boring 1-in.-dia. holes in the rails first, then cutting through the rails to the holes to form the notches. The foot rest notch (shown) is angled 45° on the seat rail, while the back rest notches are perpendicular.

PHOTO B: Fasten the leg assemblies to the seat rails with 2½-in. galvanized deck screws. Be sure the foot rest notches on the seat rails face down on your worksurface when you fasten the legs to the rails. Check the leg assemblies with a square to be sure they are perpendicular to the rails before driving the screws.

point for the 1⅛-in.-dia. hole is ¹⁵⁄₁₆ in. from the top edge of the rails. Drill the holes, then form the notches by drawing a pair of lines from each hole perpendicular to the top edge of the rails. Cut along the lines to form the two notches.

BUILD & ATTACH THE LEG ASSEMBLIES TO THE SEAT RAILS

❸ Cut the six legs to length. Draw and cut 1¾-in. radiuses on both ends of the two foot rest legs and on one end of the four seat section legs.

❹ Cut the seat stretchers to length. Mark the stretcher locations on the inside faces of the four seat section legs. Center the stretchers on the width of the legs. The top edges of the stretchers are 3½ in. down from the square ends of the legs. Clamp the parts together and fasten the legs to the seat stretchers with countersunk 3-in. galvanized deck screws.

❺ Attach the leg assemblies to the seat rails. Fasten one leg assembly 6½ in. from the ends of the rails with the foot rest notches using 2½-in. deck screws. Attach the second leg assembly so the span between the outside faces of the seat stretchers is 46 in. (**See Photo B**).

INSTALL THE BACK SUPPORTS
❻ Measure and cut the two back supports to length.

❼ Rout the three back rest grooves in each back support. Refer to the measurements on the *Back Supports* drawing, page 117, to determine the groove locations. Clamp the back supports side by side so you can mark and gang-cut slots on both supports at one time. Then rout the grooves with a ¾-in. core box bit. Cut the slots in multiple passes to keep from overloading the router bit (**See Photo C**).

❽ Attach the back supports to the tops of the seat stretchers. Leave a 4½-in. space between the supports and the legs (See *Head End View*, page 117) to allow ample room for the back rails and adjustment braces. Align the ends of the back supports so they are flush with the outside faces of the seat stretchers. Drill pilot holes, and fasten the parts with 3-in. galvanized deck screws (**See Photo D**).

PHOTO C: Gang-rout notches in the back supports to ensure that the notches will line up perfectly on both pieces. Use a ¾-in. core box bit, and cut the notches in several passes of increasing depth. We clamped a short T-square style straightedge jig to guide the router when cutting.

PHOTO D: Fasten the back supports to the seat stretchers. Leave 4½-in. spaces between the back supports and the legs to provide clearance for the chair back rails and adjustment braces.

PHOTO E: Cut the 19 seat slats to length, and ease the top edges and ends of each slat with a ½-in. roundover bit in the router. We used a plywood jig clamped to the benchtop to "frame" each slat on all sides and hold it steady while routing. This way, the slats require no further clamping.

PHOTO F: Screw the five seat slats to the seat rails. Determine and mark the positions of the end slats first, then space the remaining three slats evenly between the end slats. If the slat space is consistent on your chair, use a scrap spacer to make spacing easy when fastening the parts.

PHOTO G: Bore a 1-in.-dia. hole through each back rail for the back rest dowel and a ³⁄₈-in.-deep counterbore for the heads and washers of the adjustment brace pivot bolts.

CUT & ATTACH THE SLATS

9 Cut all the slats to length. Cut one slat 3¼ in. shorter than the others so it can fit between the seat rails when the back rest is inclined.

10 Rout a ½-in. roundover on the face edges of the slats. We made a plywood jig and clamped it to our worksurface to hold each slat steady for routing (**See Photo E**).

11 Attach the five slats that make up the fixed seat of the chair to the seat rails. First mark the positions of the two end slats. Locate the edge of the slat closest to the foot rest notch by measuring 1¾ in. from the foot end of the seat rails and marking a line. Then measure 19½ in. from this line to locate the edge closest to the back rest notch. Space the remaining three slats evenly between the end slats. NOTE: *The spacing between the slats will vary, depending upon the width of your slat stock. What is most important is that all the slats fit between the marks you've just drawn on the seat rails.* Fasten the slats to the rails with 2½-in. deck screws (**See Photo F**).

BUILD THE BACK REST

12 Rip and crosscut the two adjustment braces to size, and cut ¾-in. radiuses on both ends of each part. Drill one end for a ³⁄₈-in.-dia. pivot bolt and the other end for the ¾-in.-dia. adjustment dowel. Bore the holes at the centerpoints you established for marking the end radiuses.

13 Cut the back rails to length, then miter-cut one end at a 60° angle. Cut a 1¾-in. radius on one corner of the other end of the rails with a jig saw as shown in the *Back Rails* drawing, page 117.

⑭ Bore holes in the back rails for the back rest dowel and adjustment brace pivot bolts. Refer to the *Back Rails* drawing, page 117, for locating these hole positions. Clamp each rail to your worksurface. Bore a 1-in.-dia. hole through the radiused ends of the rails for the back rest dowel. Using the same bit, drill a ⅜-in.-deep counterbore for the pivot bolt head and washer (**See Photo G**).

⑮ Drill a ⅜-in.-dia. hole through the back rails for the adjustment brace pivot bolts in the center of the counterbores you drilled in Step 14 (**See Photo H**).

⑯ Install the adjustment dowel in the adjustment braces. Cut the ¾-in.-dia. dowel to length, and fasten the dowel into the holes in the adjustment braces with 4d galvanized finish nails.

⑰ Attach the slats to the back rails. On the seven full-length slats, drill a line of countersunk pilot holes 4¼ in. from each end. On the short slat, drill the pilot holes 1⅛ in. from each end. Attach the end slats first. Align the short slat so it is even with the radiused ends of the back rails, and overhang the upper slat ½ in. beyond the angled ends. Make sure these two slats are square with the rails and that the inside faces of the rails are 14 in. apart. Screw these first two slats in place. Then space and attach the six intermediate slats evenly between the end slats.

⑱ Cut the 1-in.-dia. back rest dowel to length. Slide it through the holes in the back rails, overhang the ends evenly and fasten the dowel in place with a 6d galvanized nail at each end (**See Photo I**). Drill pilot holes to keep the nails from splitting the dowels.

PHOTO H: Drill ⅜-in.-dia. holes through the back rails, centered on the 1-in.-dia. counterbore holes. These holes will house pivot bolts for the adjustment brace that supports the chair back and holds it in one of three positions.

PHOTO I: Tack the back rest dowel in place on the back rest rails with #6d galvanized finish nails. Drive the nails through the rails and into the dowels. To keep the dowels from splitting, drill a pilot hole for the nails first.

PHOTO J: Install the adjustment brace to the back rest with bolts, washers and nuts. Place a washer on either side of each adjustment brace. Thread two nuts on each bolt and tighten the nuts against one another to lock them together, yet allow the adjustment brace to swing freely.

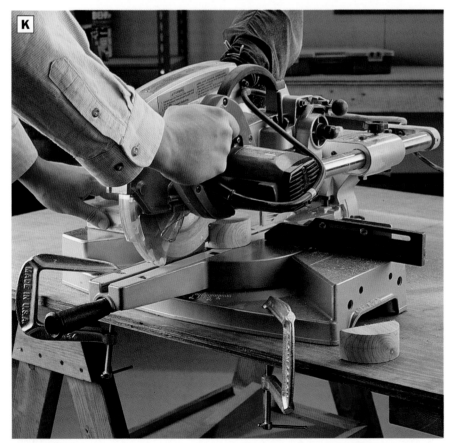

PHOTO K: Cut 1¾-in. radiuses on either end of a section of 2 × 4 cedar. Cut off these curved ends with a power miter saw or radial-arm saw. The pieces will serve as leg stops on the foot rest. Cutting short workpieces from longer stock keeps your hands a safe distance from the blade.

19 Secure the adjustment brace assembly to the back rest rails with bolts, washers and double nuts (**See Photo J**). Leave enough play when tightening the nuts against one another so the brace assembly swings freely.

ASSEMBLE THE FOOT REST

20 Cut the foot rest rails to length, then round off both ends with 1¾-in. radiuses.

21 Bore holes through the foot rest rails for the foot rest dowel and the leg pivot bolts. Locate the centerpoints for the holes using the *Foot Rest Rails* drawing, page 117. Drill a 1-in.-dia. hole through one end for the foot rest dowel. Using the same bit, drill a ⅜-in.-deep counterbore in the other end for the pivot bolt head and washer.

22 Make and attach the two leg stops. Cut 1¾-in. radiuses on both ends of a piece of 2 × 4 cedar scrap, then cut off these two semi-circles (**See Photo K**). Fasten the leg stops to the pivot bolt ends of the foot rest rails with screws.

23 Drill the ⅜-in.-dia. holes for the pivot bolts. Clamp a foot rest leg in place beneath a rail on your work-surface. Drill a ⅜-in.-dia. hole through the center of the counter-bore in the rail and through the leg (**See Photo L**). Repeat the process for the other rail and leg.

24 Cut the foot rest stretcher to length and fasten it to the legs. Center the stretcher on the width of the legs, and position the bottom edge 6 in. from the bottoms of the legs. Drill countersunk pilot holes and fasten the parts with 2½-in. galvanized deck screws.

25 Attach six slats to the foot rest rails. Drill countersunk pilot holes

PHOTO L: Drill holes through the foot rest rails and the legs. The parts will attach with bolts so the legs can pivot on the rails.

2¼ in. from each end of the slats. Attach the end slats first. Locate one slat 1¾ in. from the leg ends of the short rails. Set the other end slat 2¼ in. from the dowel-hole ends of the rails. Make sure the framework is square. Then fasten the intermediate slats evenly between the end slats.

26 Cut and attach the foot rest dowel to the rails with 6d finish nails. The dowel should overhang the rails evenly on both sides.

27 Attach the leg assembly to the foot rest rails with ⅜-in.-dia. bolts, washers and double nuts (**See Photo M**).

FINISHING TOUCHES

28 Ease all chair edges thoroughly with sandpaper (**See Photo N**). Stain and/or seal as desired. We applied a clear exterior sealer to highlight the beauty of the cedar, but this project could be stained, painted or left unfinished.

PHOTO M: Attach the foot rest stretcher to the legs with 2½-in. deck screws, then join the leg assembly to the foot rest with bolts, washers and double nuts.

PHOTO N: Set the back and foot rests in place on the seat, and test the action of the parts. Then sand all exposed surfaces of the chair with medium-grit sandpaper. If you sand in an enclosed place, wear a particle mask. Cedar dust can be irritating to your nose and lungs.

Woven Wood Deck Chair

Outdoor furniture should be as fun to build as it is functional to own—and this unique deck chair accomplishes both purposes. You'll build the chair frame and legs entirely from exterior plywood for durability, and assemble the major components with threaded metal inserts. Then, try your hand at weaving when you construct the seat and back lattice from bending plywood. As far as comfort is concerned, the woven seat and back provide just enough "give" to make cushions unnecessary. You could build several of these chairs and paint them in a variety of bright colors to add a festive flair to any patio or deck.

Vital Statistics: Woven Wood Deck Chair

TYPE: Woven wood deck chair

OVERALL SIZE: 32H × 32D × 25W

MATERIAL: Exterior plywood, bending plywood

JOINERY: Butt joints reinforced with galvanized screws or threaded inserts and brass machine screws

CONSTRUCTION DETAILS:

· Threaded inserts allow the chair to be disassembled for storage
· Seat and back are woven from thin, bending plywood strips captured in rabbeted frames
· Frame parts laminated from two layers of 3/4-in. plywood for strength

FINISHING OPTIONS: Exterior latex primer and paint, exterior spar varnish

Building time

 PREPARING STOCK
0 hours

 LAYOUT
4-5 hours

 CUTTING PARTS
2-4 hours

 ASSEMBLY
6-8 hours

 FINISHING
2-3 hours

TOTAL: 14-20 hours

Tools you'll use

· Table saw
· Jig saw
· Router table with 1/2-in. flush-trimming bit, 1/2-in. straight bit, 3/8-in. roundover bit
· Right-angle drilling guide
· Drill/driver
· Compass
· Clamps
· Drum sander
· Combination square
· Fine-tooth backsaw

Shopping list

☐ (1) 3/4 in. × 4 × 8 ft. exterior plywood

☐ (1) 1/8 in. × 2 × 4 ft. bending plywood

☐ (4) 1/4 × 4-in. flathead brass machine screws, washers, nuts

☐ (12) 1/4 × 2-in. flathead brass machine screws

☐ (12) 1/4 × 1/2-in. threaded inserts

☐ #8 galvanized flathead wood screws (1/2-, 11/4-in.)

☐ Two-part epoxy

☐ Moisture-resistant wood glue

☐ Exterior spar varnish

☐ Exterior latex primer, paint

Deck Chair

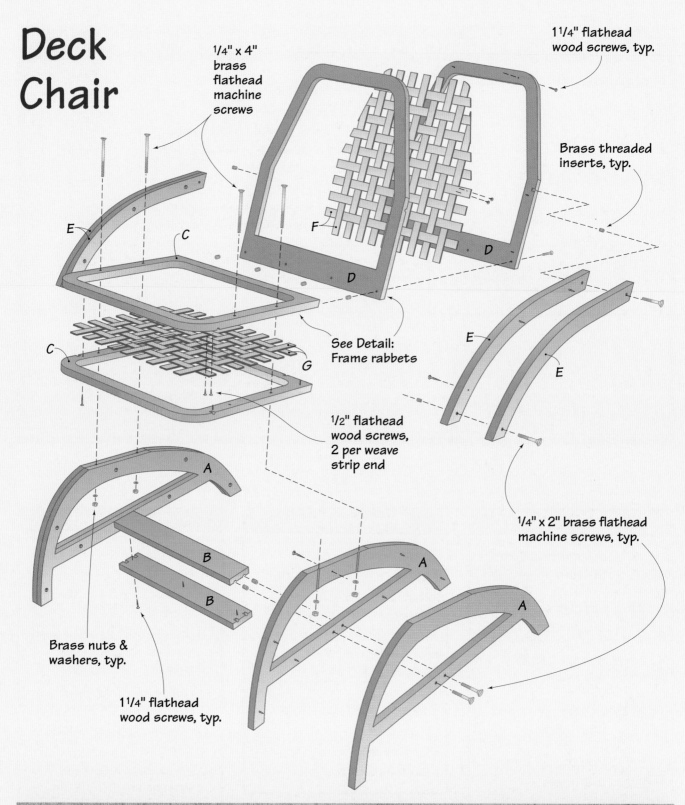

1/4" x 4" brass flathead machine screws

1 1/4" flathead wood screws, typ.

Brass threaded inserts, typ.

E

C

F

D

D

D

E

E

C

See Detail: Frame rabbets

G

1/2" flathead wood screws, 2 per weave strip end

1/4" x 2" brass flathead machine screws, typ.

A

B

B

A

A

Brass nuts & washers, typ.

1 1/4" flathead wood screws, typ.

Woven Wood Deck Chair Cutting List

Part	No.	Size	Material	Part	No.	Size	Material
A. Legs	4	$3/4 \times 13 \times 32$ in.	Exterior ply	**E.** Arms	4	$3/4 \times 7 1/2 \times 22$ in.	Exterior ply
B. Leg stretchers	2	$3/4 \times 3 \times 19$ in.	"	**F.** Back weave	18	$1/8 \times 1 \times 21$ in.	Bending ply
C. Seat frames	2	$3/4 \times 22 \times 18 1/4$ in.	"	**G.** Seat weave	7	$1/8 \times 1 \times 21$ in.	"
D. Back frames	2	$3/4 \times 22 \times 23 1/2$ in.	"		9	$1/8 \times 1 \times 17 1/4$ in.	"

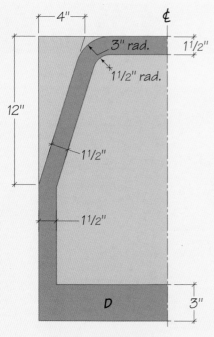

BACK FRAMES

4"
3" rad.
1¹/₂"
1¹/₂" rad.
12"
1¹/₂"
1¹/₂"
D
3"

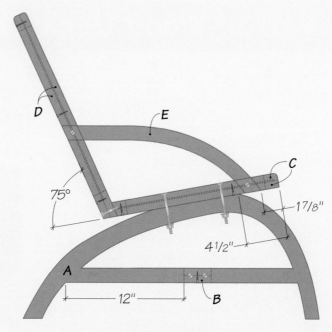

SIDE VIEW

D
E
C
75°
17/8"
4¹/₂"
A
B
12"

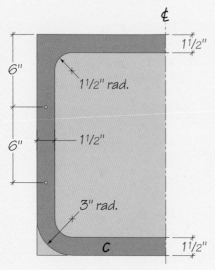

SEAT FRAMES

1¹/₂"
6"
1¹/₂" rad.
1¹/₂"
6"
3" rad.
C
1¹/₂"

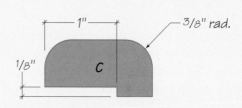

DETAIL: FRAME RABBETS

1"
3/8" rad.
1/8"
C

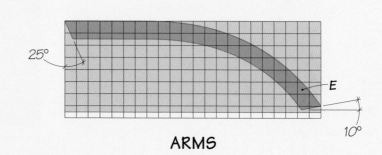

ARMS

25°
E
10°

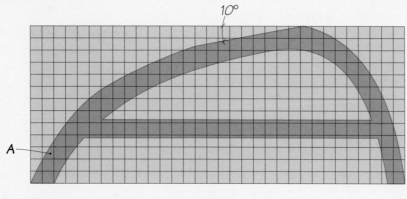

LEGS

10°
A
Grid squares
are 1" x 1"

PHOTO A: Rough-out each leg with a jig saw, then screw a hardboard leg template to it and rout the leg flush to the template with a flush-trimming bit on the router table. Set the bit's depth so the bearing rides along the template as you rout the leg shapes.

MAKE THE LEGS

1 Enlarge the leg pattern from the *Legs* drawing, page 127, to full size and use it to make a template from ¼-in. hardboard. Sand the cut edges smooth.

2 Rough-out the leg shapes. Cut four rectangular leg blanks to size from exterior plywood. Using the leg template as a guide, trace about ¼ in. outside the template profiles onto each leg workpiece, and cut the legs to rough shape with a jig saw.

3 Trim the legs to final shape. Screw the leg template temporarily to each of the legs with countersunk screws, and trim the legs to final shape with a piloted flush-trimming bit on the router table **(See Photo A)**.

4 Fasten pairs of legs together with moisture-resistant wood glue and countersunk 1¼-in. flathead wood screws to make two double-thick legs.

5 Cut the leg stretchers to size and shape, and laminate them together with glue and 1¼-in. screws to form one thick stretcher.

6 Clamp the stretcher between the legs and drill for threaded inserts. See the *Side View* drawing, page 127, for stretcher placement. Drill two countersunk ¼-in.-dia. holes through each leg and about ⅝ in. deep into both ends of the stretcher **(See Photo B)**. Center the holes on the thickness of the stretcher, and lay them out so they are spaced 1½ in. apart. Unclamp the leg assembly and redrill the holes in the ends of the stretcher to the manufacturer's recommended diameter for fitting the threaded inserts.

7 Twist the threaded inserts into the holes in the stretcher with a large screwdriver, using a dab of two-part epoxy to secure each insert in place **(See Photo C)**. Then assemble the legs and stretcher with 2-in. flathead brass machine screws.

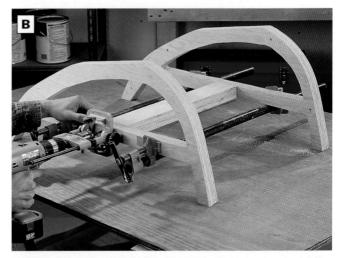

PHOTO B: Clamp the stretcher in place between the two legs, and drill ¼-in. holes through the legs and into the stretcher for threaded inserts and machine screws. A right-angle drilling guide ensures straight holes.

BUILD THE SEAT & BACK

8 Cut the seat frames and back frames to shape. Start by cutting pairs of seat and back blanks to size. Follow the dimensions given in the *Back Frames* and *Seat Frames* drawings, page 127, to lay out one back frame and one seat frame. Use a combination square to mark centerpoints for drawing the 1½- and 3-in.-radiused corners on these parts, and scribe the curves with a compass. Cut out the back frame and seat frame with a jig saw, and smooth the cut edges with a sander. Then use these two frame pieces as

PHOTO C: After enlarging the stretcher holes to the proper diameter for the threaded inserts, screw in the inserts. A dab of two-part epoxy in each stretcher hole will lock the inserts in place.

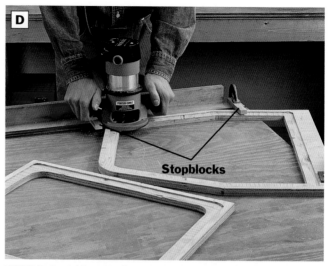

PHOTO D: Rout 1-in.-wide, 1/8-in.-deep rabbets into the face of one seat and back frame. A shop-made jig insets the rabbet correctly from the edge of the frames, and stopblocks on the jig limit the router's path.

patterns to help you cut the other back and seat frame to match. Save the center cutouts; they can be used as material for the arms later.

❾ Rout the back and seat rabbets. The woven plywood seat and back supports will be captured between the pairs of back and seat frames, which will fasten flush against one another. In order to do this, one member of each frame needs a shallow rabbet cut to accommodate the thickness of the plywood weave strips. However, the rabbet is too wide (1 in.) to rout with a piloted rabbet bit directly against the inside edges of the frames, so you'll need to build a jig from scrap 3/4-in. wood to guide the cuts. (See the tint box, below, for information on building the jig.) Mark outlines for the rabbets onto one seat and back frame piece. Clamp the rabbeting jig at both ends along the edge of your bench. Butt one edge of a seat or back frame against the jig. Resting the router base on the jig and the frame, clamp scrap wood stopblocks onto the jig so they'll limit the path of the router to stay

within your marked area. Plan to make the first round of rabbet cuts, machining one straight portion of the frames at a time. NOTE: *You'll have to reset the stopblocks to make each rabbet cut around the frame. Also, on the lower, straight edge of the back frame, insert a 2-in.-wide spacer strip between the jig's fence and the router base to offset the cut properly.* Set the bit depth to 1/8 in., and make the first of two cuts around each frame. Then, move the router base away from the jig's back and make a second pass around the frames to remove the rest of the material, widening the rabbet to 1 in. **(See Photo D)**. Round the radiused corners of the rabbets by carefully running the router along your rabbet layout lines by hand. Or, if you prefer, trim these curves with a sharp chisel.

❿ Use a 3/8-in. roundover bit in the router to ease the inside and outside edges of the rabbeted seat and back frames as well as the outside edges of the other back frame. The straight, square edge of each frame where the seat and back meet does not get routed.

WEAVE THE SEAT & BACK FRAMES

⓫ Cut the seat weave and back weave strips to size. Cut up a few extra in case you break or miscut a few when weaving. Seal all surfaces of the strips with several coats of exterior spar varnish **(See Photo E)**. Varnish the rabbeted areas on the frames as well.

⓬ Weave the seat. Begin by attaching the front-to-back (17 1/4-in.) strips. Place the middle strip in the rabbet and center it from side to side. Hold down one end with a spring clamp and fasten the other end with two countersunk 1/2-in. flathead screws. Attach

---

ROUTER RABBETING JIG

Cut two wood strips 3 in. wide and 24 and 26 in. long. Screw them together to create an L-shaped bracket with the longer strip (it will be the jig's base) overhanging the shorter one (the fence) evenly at both ends. Install a 1/2-in. straight bit in your router. Measure the distance from the outside edge of the router base to the bit, and rip the jig's base down on the table saw so that when the router is placed against the jig's fence, the bit clears the jig base by 1/2 in.

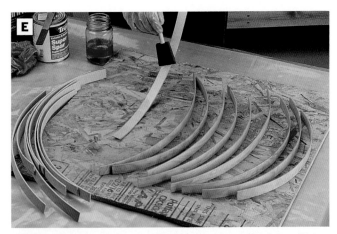

PHOTO E: Seal all surfaces of the seat and back weaving strips with two coats of spar varnish. Varnish the rabbets on the seat and back frames as well as the mating surfaces on the other seat and back frame.

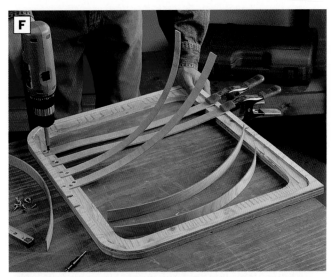

PHOTO F: Fasten one end of the middle seat weave strip with screws while holding the other end with a spring clamp in the rabbet. Once the strip is fastened on one end, remove the clamp. Attach the remaining front-to-back strips in the same way, spacing them 1 in. apart.

PHOTO G: After screwing down both ends of the first four cross strips on the back frame, continue weaving in the rest of the cross strips with their ends free. Then trim the weave to fit into the angled portions of the frame and screw the strips down one at a time.

the other weave strips working outward from the center strip, screwing one end of each strip to the frame 1 in. apart **(See Photo F)**. Remove all the spring clamps so the ends of the strips are free. Then attach the side-to-side (21-in.) cross strips. Weave the first cross strip through the attached strips on the frame, starting down near their fixed ends, going over and under all the way across. Adjust the strip so there is an even 1⅛-in. gap between it and the inside edge of the frame, and fasten it into the rabbet at each end with two countersunk ½-in. flathead screws. Continue weaving cross strips up the seat, alternating which way you start weaving each strip to form a lattice. You should use seven strips. Space the strips 1 in. apart, with 1⅛-in. spaces between the outermost strips and the frame. Once the weave is complete, screw down the free ends of the front-to-back strips.

🄓 Weave the back frame. This time, attach the first set of strips (running vertically on the frame) at the lower end of the frame. As you work your way outward from the center, let the strips overhang the angled and corner sections of the frame. Weave the cross strips in, starting at the bottom of the frame. Make all the gaps a consistent 1 in. Attach the bottom four cross strips at both ends in the rabbet. Let the remaining cross strips overhang the angled portions of the frame, and continue weaving all the way up the frame with the strips loose. Then trim the overhanging strips to fit into the rabbet **(See Photo G)**. Cut the vertical strips to fit into the rabbets as well, and screw them down to complete the back.

🄔 Assemble the back and seat frames. In the angled sections of the rabbeted back frame, the weaving strips overlap in some areas, doubling their thickness. In order to be able to screw the back frames together so they fit flush, you'll need to notch out these areas in the unrabbeted back frame. Set the back frame pieces together and mark spots on the unrabbeted frame that will need to be notched **(See Photo H)**. Pare away ⅛ in. of material in these areas until the two frames fit snugly together. Assemble the back and seat frames with countersunk 1¼-in. screws.

ATTACH THE BACK FRAME TO THE SEAT FRAME
🄕 Cut a 15° bevel along the straight edge of the chair back and seat on the table saw **(See Photo I)**. This will create the joint where the two frames meet.

🄖 Use a combination square to draw a line along the rear face of the back frame, ⅝ in. from the bottom (beveled) edge. Mark points along this line at 1 in. and 7 in. from each side of the frame. Clamp the back frame to the seat frame as shown in the *Side View* drawing, page 127, with the bottom edge of the back frame flush with the bottom of the seat frame. Drill countersunk ¼-in. machine screw holes perpendicular to the back frame at the marked points. Use a depth stop or a piece of tape wrapped around the bit to drill the holes 2 in. deep. Separate the frames and enlarge the holes in the seat frame to accept four threaded inserts. Use epoxy when you screw the inserts into the seat frame. Fasten the back frame to the seat frame with 2-in. flathead machine screws.

ASSEMBLE THE CHAIR

17 Make the arms. Follow the *Arms* grid drawing, page 127, to lay out and cut one arm to size. Use this workpiece as a template for cutting the other three arm pieces. Then laminate pairs of arms together with glue and 1¼-in. flathead wood screws to form two arms.

18 Attach the seat to the legs. Use a combination square to draw a line along the top face of each side of the seat frame, ¾ in. from the edges. Mark two points along these lines 6 in. and 12 in. from the back edge of the seat frame. Place the seat assembly on the leg assembly, and align them so the front edge of the seat overhangs the flat section of the legs by 4½ in. Clamp the seat to the legs with their sides flush. Drill ¼-in.-dia. countersunk holes all the way through the seat frame and legs at the four marked points. Fasten the seat to the legs with 4-in. brass machine screws, nuts and washers.

19 Install the arms. The front edge of each arm should be about 1⅞ in. from the front edge of the seat frame. Pivot the arms at this point until the back edges of the arms align with the back face of the chair back. Clamp the arms in place and drill a countersunk ¼-in.-dia. hole, 2 in. deep, where each arm intersects the back and seat frames. Remove the arms, drill and install threaded inserts and attach the arms to the seat and back frames with 2-in. brass machine screws **(See Photo J)**.

FINISHING TOUCHES

20 Sand the unvarnished chair surfaces smooth and ease all sharp edges. Tape off and cover the varnished weaving with newspaper to protect it from paint. Prime all bare wood parts, and topcoat the chair with several coats of high-quality exterior latex paint.

PHOTO H: Mark the unrabbeted back frame in those areas that will need to fit around doubled-up weave strips. Remove this frame piece and notch out the marked areas with a sharp chisel.

PHOTO I: With the table saw blade tilted to 15°, cut a beveled edge on the seat and back frames where they will meet each other at an angle.

PHOTO J: Clamp the arm in position and connect it to the seat and back with 2-in. machine screws installed in threaded inserts.

Utility Cart

Asturdy, well-designed utility cart can make your lawn and garden work safer, more efficient and maybe even more enjoyable. Our cart is easy to construct from basic materials but rugged enough to give you years of hard-working service. The large, 14-in. wheels enable this cart to roll easily over bumpy ground, even while loaded to the brim with garden supplies and tools. When not in use, just stand it on end or lay it on its side against your garage or shed wall until you need it next.

Vital Statistics: Utility Cart

TYPE: Utility cart

OVERALL SIZE: 30W by 78L by 28H

MATERIAL: Exterior plywood, treated lumber

JOINERY: Butt joints reinforced with galvanized deck screws

CONSTRUCTION DETAILS:

- Dimension lumber and exposed screws for ease of construction
- Notches in cart back and crosspiece for carrying tools
- Broad wheel base for stability
- Large wheels for ease of moving heavy loads over uneven ground
- Handles cut into profiles at the ends to provide comfortable grip

FINISHING OPTIONS: Leave unfinished or topcoat with penetrating UV protectant sealer or paint if cart is stored outside

Building time

PREPARING STOCK
0 hours

LAYOUT
1-2 hours

CUTTING PARTS
2-4 hours

ASSEMBLY
2-4 hours

FINISHING
1-2 hours (optional)

TOTAL: 6-12 hours

Tools you'll use

- Circular saw
- Jig saw
- Drill/driver
- Drill press
- Right-angle drill guide
- Router with 1/2-in. roundover bit
- Combination square
- Clamps

Shopping list

- ☐ (1) $3/4$ in. × 4 ft. × 8 ft. exterior plywood
- ☐ (3) 2 × 4 in. × 8 ft. treated lumber
- ☐ Galvanized deck screws ($1^{5}/8$-, 2-, 3-in.)
- ☐ (1) $1/2$-in.-dia. × 36-in. steel rod
- ☐ (4) $1/2$-in. washers
- ☐ (2) 14-in.-dia. wheels with $1/2$-in. arbors
- ☐ (2) Cotter pins
- ☐ UV protectant sealer

Utility Cart

1/2"-rad. rounded over edges

G

F

A

B

D

E

C

E

A

F

H

3" galvanized deck screws

1/2"-dia. steel rod; length is based on thickness of wheels

1⁵/₈" galvanized deck screws, typ.

1/2" washers

Cotter pins

14"-dia. wheels with 1/2"-dia. arbors

Utility Cart Cutting List

Part	No.	Size	Material	Part	No.	Size	Material
A. Sides	2	$3/4 \times 15 \times 48$ in.	Exterior plywood	**E.** Struts	3	$1^1/2 \times 3^1/2 \times 25^1/2$ in.	Treated lumber
B. Back	1	$3/4 \times 15 \times 25^1/2$ in.	"	**F.** Handles	2	$1^1/2 \times 3^1/2 \times 64$ in.	"
C. Front	1	$3/4 \times 16^1/4 \times 25^1/2$ in.	"	**G.** Crosspiece	1	$1^1/2 \times 3^1/2 \times 27$ in.	"
D. Bottom	1	$3/4 \times 25^1/2 \times 41^1/4$ in.	"	**H.** Legs	2	$1^1/2 \times 3^1/2 \times 13$ in.	"

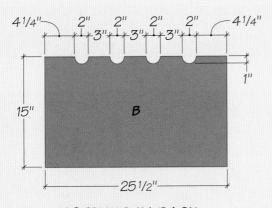

4 1/4" 2" 2" 2" 2" 4 1/4"
3" 3" 3"

15"

B

1"

25 1/2"

NOTCHES IN BACK

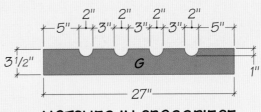

2" 2" 2" 2"
5" 3" 3" 3" 5"

3 1/2"

G

1"

27"

NOTCHES IN CROSSPIECE

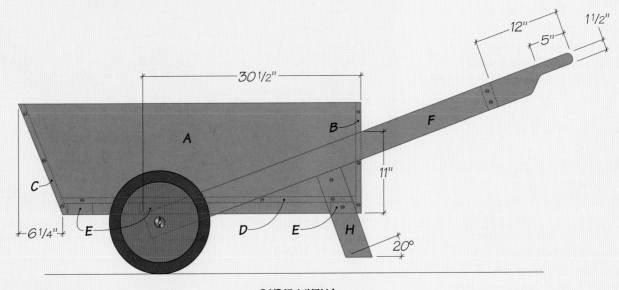

30 1/2"

12" 5" 1 1/2"

A

B

F

11"

C

6 1/4"

E

E

D

E

H

20°

SIDE VIEW

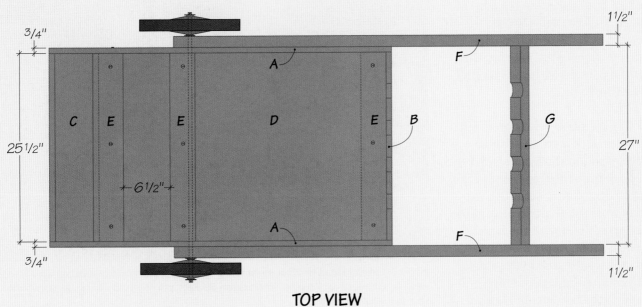

3/4"

1 1/2"

C E E D E B A F G

25 1/2" 27"

6 1/2"

A F

3/4" 1 1/2"

TOP VIEW

PHOTO A: Lay out and draw four 2-in.-dia. semicircular tool notches in the top edge of the cart back. Cut out the notches with a jig saw. Clamp the workpiece to your bench to hold it steady while you make the notched cuts.

BUILD THE BOX

The cart box is constructed of ¾-in. exterior plywood, which resists delaminating when exposed to moisture. The front of the box is angled for easy dumping, and the bottom is reinforced with three recessed 2 × 4 struts.

❶ Cut the box sides, back, front and bottom pieces to the sizes given in the *Cutting List,* page 134. Use a circular saw or jig saw guided against a clamped straightedge to cut the parts. Lay out all the parts on the plywood sheet before cutting any workpieces to ensure that you will cut the sheet efficiently and minimize waste.

❷ Mark and cut the four notches for tool handles in the top edge of the back piece. Refer to the *Notches in Back* drawing, page 135, for spacing the notches. Cut out the notches with your jig saw **(See Photo A)**.

❸ Cut the three struts to length and attach them to the bottom piece. Position the front strut 1½ in. back from the front edge of the bottom, the center strut 6½ in. away from the front strut, and the rear strut flush with the back edge of the bottom. Apply moisture-resistant wood glue to the struts, drill countersunk pilot holes through the bottom, and fasten

PHOTO B: Cut and install the three struts to the cart bottom with moisture-resistant wood glue and 2-in. galvanized deck screws. For maximum strength, use at least six screws to fasten each strut to the bottom panel.

136

PHOTO C: Build the cart box. Fasten the cart back to the bottom, then screw the sides to the back and bottom. Install the cart front last. Strengthen the joints with glue when you attach the parts.

PHOTO D: Mark and cut the grip profiles on the handles. Ease the sharp edges on the grips by rounding them over with a router and ½-in. roundover bit.

the struts with 1⅝-in. screws (**See Photo B**).

❹ Lay out and cut the angled front ends of the side pieces. Make a mark along the bottom edge of each side piece 6¼ in. from one end. Draw a straight line from these marks to the corner of the top edge. Cut along these angled lines.

❺ Bevel-cut the top edge of the front piece. Set the base of your circular saw to 22½°, and trim along the top edge so it will be flush when fastened between the angled front edges of the sides. The bottom edge will be hidden, so there's no need to bevel-cut it to match.

❻ Bevel-cut the front edge of the bottom piece.

❼ Assemble the box with glue and 1⅝-in. galvanized deck screws. Drill countersunk pilot holes in the sides, front and back. First, attach the back to the bottom, driving screws through the back and into the back strut. Next, attach the sides to the bottom and the back (**See Photo C**). Align the bottoms of the sides with the bottoms of the struts. The back edges of the sides overlap the back. Finally, attach the front to the bottom and sides, making sure that the angled edge is flush with the top edges of the sides.

ATTACH THE HANDLES, LEGS & CROSSPIECE
The handles, legs and crosspiece are made of treated lumber. When handling chemically-treated lumber, it is a good idea to protect your skin by wearing work gloves. Also, work in a well-ventilated area when cutting this wood.

❽ Cut the handles to length from 2 × 4 stock.

❾ Shape the grips on the handles. Following the *Side View* drawing, page 135, mark the grip profiles and cut the shapes with your jig saw. Use your router with a ½-in. roundover bit to ease the sharp edges on the grips (**See Photo D**). This step can also be done with a rasp and sandpaper, or a handheld belt sander if you don't have a router.

❿ Position and attach the handles. Mark the location of the handles on the box sides by measuring from the back corner up 11 in. and forward 30½ in. Draw a straight line between these points on both sides. Drill a line of pilot holes 1¾ in. down from these lines, and countersink the holes from inside the box. Position the handles so the top edges align with the diagonal marks on the cart. Apply moisture-resistant wood glue, clamp the first handle in place, and attach the

PHOTO E: Mark the locations of the handles on the cart box, and install the handles with moisture-resistant wood glue and 2-in. galvanized deck screws. Clamp the handles in place as you attach them.

PHOTO F: Clamp the crosspiece in position between the handles, drill countersunk pilot holes through the parts, and fasten the crosspiece to the handles with 3-in. galvanized deck screws.

handle with 2-in. screws. Flip the box over, and clamp and attach the second handle (**See Photo E**).

⑪ Cut the legs to length, then cut the bottom ends of the legs at a 20° angle. Position the legs on the cart sides so the top ends of the legs rest against the bottom edges of the handles, and the back edges of the legs align with the bottom back corners of the back struts. Fasten the legs with glue and screws.

⑫ Cut and attach the crosspiece. Cut the crosspiece to length. Mark the tool-handle notches by aligning the crosspiece flush with the top edge of the cart back and tracing the profile. Cut the notches with a jig saw. Clamp the crosspiece in position, 12 in. from the upper ends of the handles. Drill countersunk pilot holes, and screw the crosspiece in place with 3-in. galvanized deck screws (**See Photo F**).

INSTALL THE WHEELS

Wheels can be purchased in a variety of sizes. Keep in mind that wheel diameter will affect the overall height of the cart and the length of the legs. The legs should be short enough so that the cart leans back slightly when at rest; this ensures that the legs won't

be snagging on the ground as you go over bumps or down hills. Also, larger wheels will navigate uneven ground much more smoothly than will small wheels. We found 14-in. wheels to be a convenient size and readily available at our local building center.

⑬ Locate and drill the axle holes. Mark 45° lines from the bottom corners of the handles using a combination square. Drill ½-in.-dia. axle holes through the handles where the lines intersect. NOTE: *Be sure the holes clear the bottom of the center stretcher, especially if you've modified the position of the handle, based on the wheels you are using for the cart* (**See Photo G**).

⑭ Cut the axle rod to length. If your wheel hubs are 1½ in. thick, as ours were, the correct axle length will be 34½ in. If the hubs of your wheels are thicker or thinner, you will need to adjust the axle length accordingly. The axle needs to extend beyond the cart on each side ¾ in. plus the thickness of the hub to accommodate the washers and cotter pins.

⑮ Drill holes through the axle for the cotter pins. Make a wooden cradle by cutting a groove into the face of an 8- to 12-in. piece of 2 × 4 with two passes of

PHOTO G: Mark locations for the axle near the bottom ends of the handles. Then drill ½-in.-dia. holes through each handle. A right-angle drilling guide will ensure straight holes.

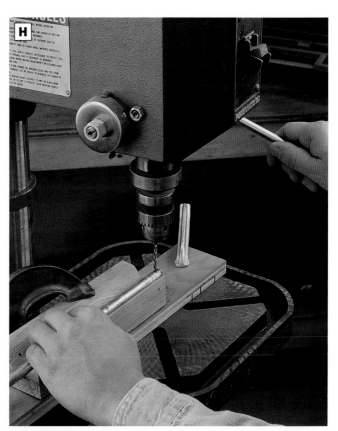

PHOTO H: Cut a V-shaped notch in a scrap of 2 × 4 to help steady the axle as you drill holes for cotter pins. Fasten the notched cradle to another scrap, and clamp the jig to the drill press table.

your saw set at a 45° angle. Fasten the grooved 2 × 4 to a larger piece of ¾-in. scrap to serve as a clamping surface. Clamp this "cradle" to your drill press table to support the axle while you drill it. Drill a ⅛-in.-dia. hole ½ in. in from each end of the axle rod (**See Photo H**).

🕦 Install the wheels. Slide the axle and wheels in place, positioning a washer on either side of each wheel. Secure the wheels by inserting cotter pins through the axle holes and bending the ends around the axle (**See Photo I**).

FINISHING TOUCHES

🕧 The exterior plywood cart box and treated lumber parts will hold up well to the knock-about use you're going to give this cart, and they require no special finish. However, if you'll store this cart outside where it is exposed to the elements, it's a good idea to give the cart a coat of primer and paint or penetrating wood sealer to protect the plywood parts. Otherwise, they could delaminate over time. TIP: *Treated lumber is often too damp to paint when you buy it. Allow the treated wood parts on the cart several weeks to dry thoroughly before painting.*

PHOTO I: Install the axle, washers and wheels on the cart. Slip cotter pins through the holes on each end of the axle, and secure the wheels by bending the ends of the cotter pins around the axle.

Basic Garden Bench

Garden benches come in many varieties, from rustic and casual to refined and formal. This casual bench is built from cedar, employing exposed screws in a construction style that's surely within the range of most weekend woodworkers. Like many of our plans, this project can be easily adapted. By simply changing the finish to bright paint or modifying the profile of the back, you'll have the perfect project to suit your personal taste or setting. It's a piece of furniture that can withstand the elements year-round and, after weathering outdoors for a bit, will look as natural in your garden as the primroses and petunias.

Vital Statistics: Basic Garden Bench

TYPE: Garden bench

OVERALL SIZE: $24^1/2$D by $59^1/2$L by 36H

MATERIAL: Cedar

JOINERY: Butt joints reinforced with galvanized deck screws

CONSTRUCTION DETAILS:
- Wide seat and modestly angled back ensure comfort
- Gentle contoured design on the back slats can be easily adapted to other shapes
- Exposed screws enhance rustic, outdoor appearance
- Assembly of three substructures—back, seat and leg/arm assemblies—simplifies construction

FINISHING OPTIONS: Penetrating UV protectant sealer or leave unfinished to weather naturally to gray

Building time

PREPARING STOCK
0 hours

LAYOUT
2-4 hours

CUTTING PARTS
2-4 hours

ASSEMBLY
4-6 hours

FINISHING
2-3 hours

TOTAL: 10-17 hours

Tools you'll use

- Circular saw or power miter saw
- Jig saw
- Drill/driver
- Clamps
- Combination square
- Carpenter's square

Shopping list

- ☐ (1) 2 × 6 in. × 4 ft. cedar
- ☐ (5) 2 × 4 in. × 8 ft. cedar
- ☐ (1) 2 × 2 in. × 4 ft. cedar
- ☐ (1) 1 × 8 in. × 4 ft. cedar
- ☐ (2) 1 × 6 in. × 8 ft. cedar
- ☐ (1) 1 × 6 in. × 6 ft. cedar
- ☐ (3) 1 × 4 in. × 8 ft. cedar
- ☐ Galvanized deck screws ($1^1/2$-, $2^1/2$-, 3-in.)
- ☐ UV protectant sealer

Basic Garden Bench

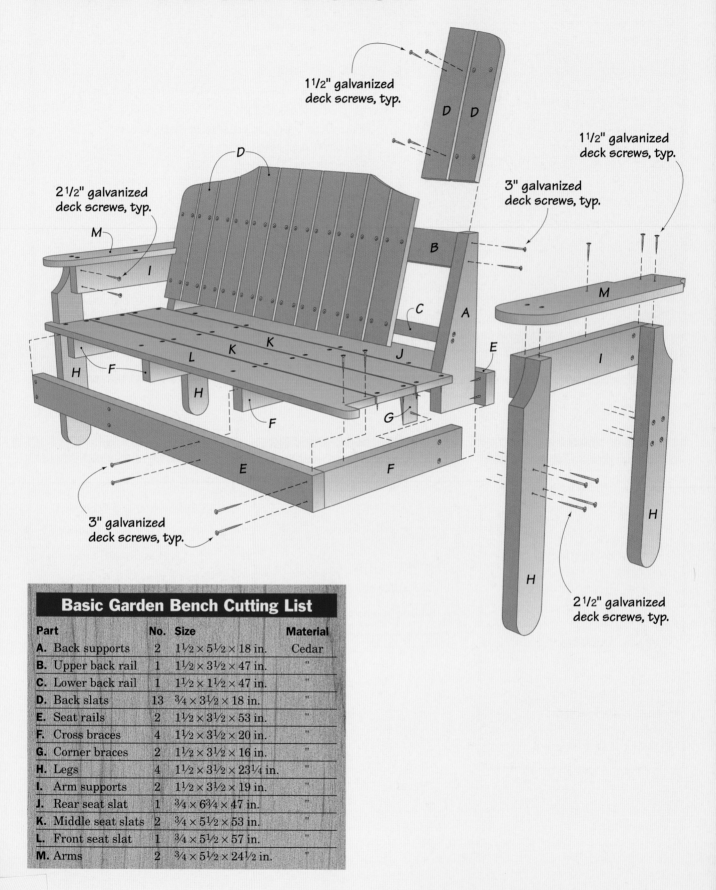

1½" galvanized deck screws, typ.

1½" galvanized deck screws, typ.

3" galvanized deck screws, typ.

2½" galvanized deck screws, typ.

2½" galvanized deck screws, typ.

3" galvanized deck screws, typ.

Basic Garden Bench Cutting List			
Part	**No.**	**Size**	**Material**
A. Back supports	2	$1\frac{1}{2} \times 5\frac{1}{2} \times 18$ in.	Cedar
B. Upper back rail	1	$1\frac{1}{2} \times 3\frac{1}{2} \times 47$ in.	"
C. Lower back rail	1	$1\frac{1}{2} \times 1\frac{1}{2} \times 47$ in.	"
D. Back slats	13	$\frac{3}{4} \times 3\frac{1}{2} \times 18$ in.	"
E. Seat rails	2	$1\frac{1}{2} \times 3\frac{1}{2} \times 53$ in.	"
F. Cross braces	4	$1\frac{1}{2} \times 3\frac{1}{2} \times 20$ in.	"
G. Corner braces	2	$1\frac{1}{2} \times 3\frac{1}{2} \times 16$ in.	"
H. Legs	4	$1\frac{1}{2} \times 3\frac{1}{2} \times 23\frac{1}{4}$ in.	"
I. Arm supports	2	$1\frac{1}{2} \times 3\frac{1}{2} \times 19$ in.	"
J. Rear seat slat	1	$\frac{3}{4} \times 6\frac{3}{4} \times 47$ in.	"
K. Middle seat slats	2	$\frac{3}{4} \times 5\frac{1}{2} \times 53$ in.	"
L. Front seat slat	1	$\frac{3}{4} \times 5\frac{1}{2} \times 57$ in.	"
M. Arms	2	$\frac{3}{4} \times 5\frac{1}{2} \times 24\frac{1}{2}$ in.	"

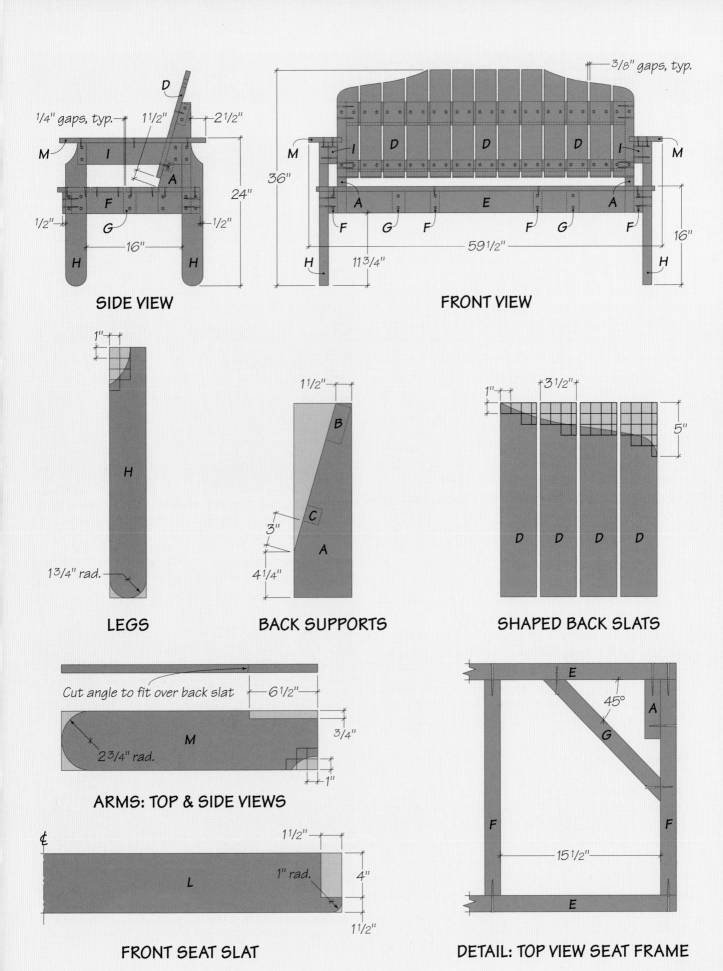

1/4" gaps, typ.　　1 1/2"　　2 1/2"

M　I　D

A

24"

1/2"　　F　　1/2"

G

H　16"　H

SIDE VIEW

3/8" gaps, typ.

M　I　D　D　D　I　M

36"

A　E　A

F　G　F　F　G　F

16"

H　11 3/4"　59 1/2"　H

FRONT VIEW

1"

H

1 3/4" rad.

LEGS

1 1/2"

B

3"

C

4 1/4"

A

BACK SUPPORTS

1"　3 1/2"

5"

D　D　D　D

SHAPED BACK SLATS

Cut angle to fit over back slat　6 1/2"

M

3/4"

2 3/4" rad.

1"

ARMS: TOP & SIDE VIEWS

¢

1 1/2"

L

1" rad.　4"

1 1/2"

FRONT SEAT SLAT

E

45°　A

G

F　F

15 1/2"

E

DETAIL: TOP VIEW SEAT FRAME

Basic Garden Bench: Step-by-step

The styling of this bench is largely determined by the profiles of the shaped pieces—the back, arms and legs. With a little thought and planning, it's possible to change all these contours without affecting the basic construction methods or dimensions of the parts. Want to express yourself with something more whimsical? Let this be your chance.

BUILD THE BACK

❶ Make the angled back supports. Cut the blanks to length from 2 × 6 cedar stock. Refer to the measurements on the *Back Supports* drawing, page 143, and mark the angles onto the back rests. Clamp each blank to your worksurface, and cut the angles with a jig saw (**See Photo A**).

❷ Install the upper and lower back rails on the back supports. Cut the upper and lower back rails to length. Clamp the rails between the back supports flush with their angled edges. The bottom rail is located 3 in. up from the bottom corner of the angled portion, and the upper rail aligns with the top angle corner. Use long clamps to hold the rails in place between the back supports while you drill counter-sunk pilot holes. Attach the parts with 3-in. galvanized deck screws.

❸ Make the back slats. Cut the slats to length from 1 × 4 stock. Lay one slat in position on the back frame and mark the center of both back rails on the slat. These marks will serve as reference points for locating the screws. Line up all the slats next to one another and extend the rail reference marks across the faces of all the slats.

❹ Attach the back slats. Position the two end slats, holding their outer edges flush with the outer faces of the back supports, and attach them with countersunk 1½-in. galvanized deck screws. Clamp a straightedge

PHOTO A: Cut the back supports to length and lay out the angled edge on both supports. Clamp the supports to your worksurface and cut along the angled layout lines with a jig saw.

PHOTO B: Establish slat positions by attaching the end slats flush to the outer edges of the back supports, then clamping a straightedge across the bottom. Use a long ³⁄₈-in.-thick spacer to position the intermediate slats as you fasten them in place.

across the lower ends of the two slats to align the ends of the remaining slats. Use a long ³⁄₈-in. spacer to establish consistent gaps between the slats, and fasten the slats to the rails with galvanized deck screws (See Photo B).

❺ Cut the profile on the back slats. You can create your own unique contour for the back, or create a hardboard template of the pattern provided in the *Shaped Back Slats* drawing, page 143. After drawing your profile along the top edge of the back slats, clamp the back assembly to your worksurface and cut the profile with a jig saw (See Photo C). Sand the cut edges smooth.

BUILD & ATTACH THE SEAT FRAME

❻ Cut the two seat rails and the four cross braces to length from 2 × 4 stock.

❼ Assemble the seat frame. Clamp the cross braces in place between the rails, with the inner braces spaced 15¹⁄₂ in. from the end braces. Drill countersunk pilot holes and fasten the rails to the braces with 3-in. galvanized deck screws (See Photo D).

❽ Cut and attach the two corner braces. Cut the braces to length and miter-cut the ends to 45° (See Photo E). Position the braces inside the back corners of the seat frame, drill countersunk pilot holes near the ends of the braces and attach the corner braces with 2¹⁄₂-in. galvanized deck screws.

❾ Fasten the back assembly to the seat frame. Stand the back assembly upright and inside the seat frame so the back supports butt against the back corners of the seat frame. Drill countersunk

PHOTO C: Once you've marked the profile (either your own design or the one we've provided in the drawings) on the back slat assembly, trim along the profile lines and smooth the cut edges.

PHOTO D: Begin assembling the seat by clamping the end cross braces between the seat rails and positioning the inner two braces 15¹⁄₂ in. from the end braces. Fasten the rails to the braces with 3-in. galvanized deck screws.

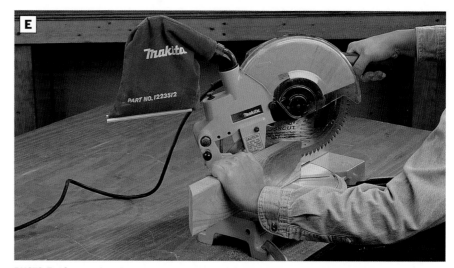

PHOTO E: After cutting the two corner braces to length, miter-cut the ends to 45°. The corner braces will fit inside the seat frames between the rails and the end cross braces.

PHOTO F: Stand the back assembly inside the seat frame behind the corner braces. Drill countersunk holes through the end cross braces and attach the back to the seat frame with countersunk deck screws.

PHOTO G: Use a compass to lay out the rounded bottom ends of the legs. Make a small hardboard template to mark the top leg profile on all four legs. Then cut the leg profiles to shape.

PHOTO H: Clamp the leg assemblies to the seat/back assembly. The bottom edge of the seat frame should be 11¾ in. up from the bottoms of the legs and extend ½ in. beyond the front legs.

pilot holes through the outer cross braces into the supports. Attach the seat frame to the back supports with 2½-in. galvanized deck screws **(See Photo F)**.

BUILD & ATTACH THE LEG ASSEMBLIES

🔟 Make the legs. Cut the legs to length, then lay out the leg profiles **(See Photo G)** following either the *Legs* pattern provided on page 143 or your own personal design. Cut the legs to shape with your jig saw and sand the cut edges smooth.

⓫ Crosscut the arm supports to length and clamp them between the legs (be sure to orient the upper leg contours correctly). Drill countersunk pilot holes and attach the supports to the legs with 2½-in. galvanized deck screws. When you fasten these parts together, check the assemblies with a carpenter's square to be sure that the legs are perpendicular to the arm supports and are parallel with one another.

⓬ Fasten the leg assemblies to the seat frame. Clamp each leg assembly in place against the ends of the seat frame, so the bottom of the seat is 11¾ in. from the bottoms of the legs, and the front edges of the front legs are held back ½ in. from the front of the seat frame. The arm supports should be positioned on the inside, so they rest against the outside face of the back supports. Drill countersunk pilot holes and fasten the leg assemblies in place with 2½-in. galvanized deck screws driven through the legs into the seat frame (**See Photo H**) and through the arm supports into the back supports.

ATTACH THE SEAT SLATS & ARMS

13 Make and attach the seat slats. Rip the rear seat slat to width from 1 × 8 stock and cut it to length. Cut the middle slats to length from 1 × 6 stock. Cut the front seat slat to length, and notch the ends to fit around the front legs, as shown in the *Front Seat Slat* drawing, page 143. Sand the cut edges smooth. Lay the slats in position on the seat frame. The outside edge of the back seat slat should be flush with the back of the seat frame. Set the front slat so it notches around the front legs. Then space the two middle slats evenly between the outside slats. Drill countersunk pilot holes and attach the slats with 1½-in. galvanized deck screws (**See Photo I**).

14 Make and attach the arms. Cut the arms to length. Referring to the drawing on page 143, lay out the arm profiles and shape them with your jig saw. Note that you'll need to bevel-cut a portion of the arm rest notch at an angle to match the angle of the seat back. Sand the cut edges smooth. Position the arms on the tops of the leg assemblies, drill countersunk pilot holes, and fasten the arms with 1½-in. galvanized deck screws (**See Photo J**).

FINISHING TOUCHES

15 Sand all edges and surfaces well, and apply the finish of your choice–stain, paint or clear UV protectant sealer.

PHOTO I: Once the seat slats have been cut to length and, in the case of the rear slat, ripped to width, sand the slats smooth. Then drill countersunk holes and secure the slats to the seat frame with deck screws. The front slat will need to be notched and shaped before it is installed.

PHOTO J: Cut the arms to size and shape and fasten them to the arm supports with countersunk screws. You'll need to cut a small beveled notch on the back inside edges of the arms so the arms can butt tightly against the outermost back slats.

Formal Garden Bench

Here is an attractive interpretation of the classic mahogany garden bench you've possibly seen in formal gardens and city parks throughout the world. Its simple lines are elegant and restrained, its proportions are comfortable, and its construction is sturdy enough to last for generations. Due to the hidden-dowel joinery and plugged screws, this stately bench has no exposed metal to cause unsightly mineral streaks or to heat up in the sun. All you see and feel is the subtle beauty of natural wood.

Vital Statistics: Formal Garden Bench

TYPE: Garden bench

OVERALL SIZE: 23¼D by 58¼L by 35H

MATERIAL: Honduras mahogany

JOINERY: Butt joints reinforced with dowels or wood screws

CONSTRUCTION DETAILS:

· Concealed joints and fasteners refine traditional outdoor bench design

· Back slats and spacers fit into dado grooves in the back rails

· Seat supports and braces contoured to make seat slats a more comfortable surface on which to sit

FINISHING OPTIONS: Penetrating UV protectant sealer or leave unfinished and allow to weather naturally to gray

---

Building time

 PREPARING STOCK
1-2 hours

 LAYOUT
3-4 hours

 CUTTING PARTS
4-6 hours

 ASSEMBLY
6-8 hours

 FINISHING
1-2 hours

TOTAL: 15-22 hours

Tools you'll use

· Table saw outfitted with a dado blade

· Band saw

· Power miter saw

· Drill press

· Doweling jig

· Drill/driver

· Router with ¼-in. roundover bit

· Flush-trimming saw

· Wooden mallet

· Pneumatic nail gun or hammer and nailset

· Clamps

· Combination square

· Trammel points or string compass

· Tape measure

Shopping list

☐ (1) 1¾ × 6 in. × 6 ft. Honduras mahogany

☐ (2) 1¾ × 2¾ in. × 8 ft. Honduras mahogany

☐ (2) 1¾ × 2 in. × 8 ft. Honduras mahogany

☐ (1) 1½ × 1½ in. × 4 ft. Honduras mahogany

☐ (1) ¾ × 2¾ in. × 4 ft. Honduras mahogany

☐ (7) ¾ × 2½ in. × 6 ft. Honduras mahogany

☐ (3) ¾ × 1¼ in. × 8 ft. Honduras mahogany

☐ Fluted dowels (⅜ × 2-in. and 5/16 × 1½-in.)

☐ Moisture-resistant wood glue

☐ Flathead wood screws (1½-in.)

Formal Garden Bench

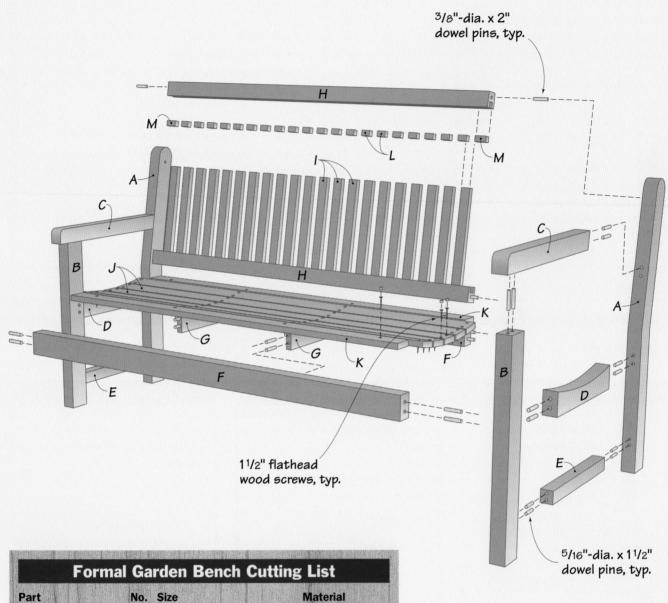

3/8"-dia. x 2"
dowel pins, typ.

H

M

L

I

A

C

B

J

D

G

H

G

K

K

F

F

E

C

A

B

D

E

5/16"-dia. x 1 1/2"
dowel pins, typ.

1 1/2" flathead
wood screws, typ.

Formal Garden Bench Cutting List

Part	No.	Size	Material
A. Back legs	2	$1^{3}/_{4} \times 5^{7}/_{8} \times 35$ in.	Honduras mahogany
B. Front legs	2	$1^{3}/_{4} \times 2^{3}/_{4} \times 23^{1}/_{4}$ in.	"
C. Arm rests	2	$1^{3}/_{4} \times 2 \times 20$ in.	"
D. Seat supports	2	$1^{3}/_{4} \times 2^{3}/_{4} \times 14^{1}/_{2}$ in.	"
E. End stretchers	2	$1^{1}/_{2} \times 1^{1}/_{2} \times 14^{1}/_{2}$ in.	"
F. Stretchers	2	$1^{3}/_{4} \times 2^{3}/_{4} \times 54^{1}/_{2}$ in.	"
G. Braces	2	$^{3}/_{4} \times 2^{3}/_{4} \times 14^{1}/_{2}$ in.	"
H. Back rails	2	$1^{3}/_{4} \times 2 \times 54^{1}/_{2}$ in.	"
I. Back slats	21	$^{3}/_{4} \times 1^{1}/_{4} \times 13^{1}/_{4}$ in.	"
J. Inner seat slats	5	$^{3}/_{4} \times 2^{1}/_{2} \times 58$ in.	"
K. Outer seat slats	2	$^{3}/_{4} \times 2^{1}/_{2} \times 54^{1}/_{2}$ in.	"
L. Short spacers	40	$^{3}/_{4} \times ^{3}/_{4} \times 1^{1}/_{4}$ in.	"
M. Long spacers	4	$^{3}/_{4} \times ^{3}/_{4} \times 1^{5}/_{8}$ in.	"

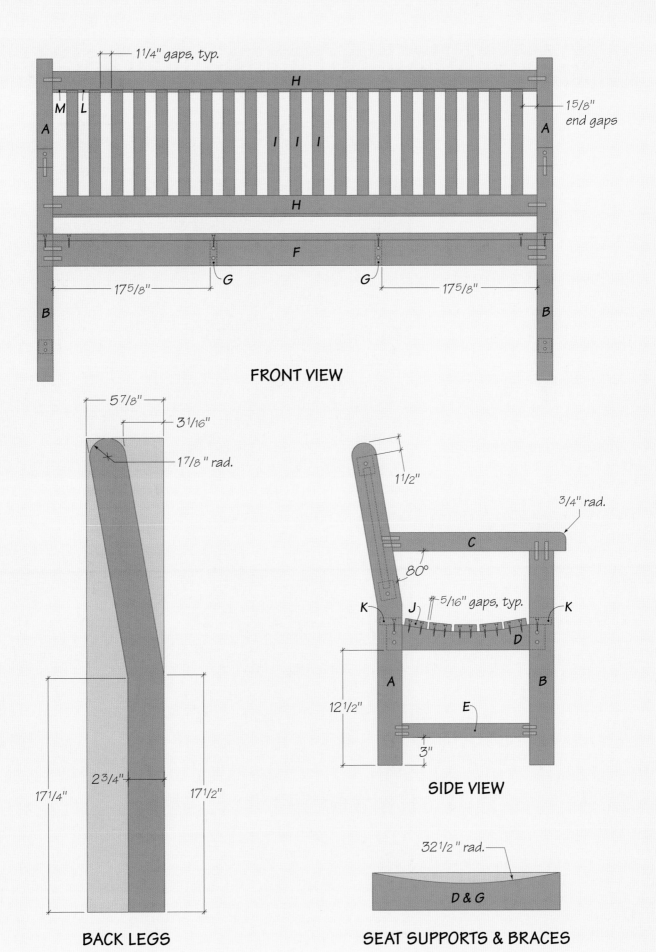

1¼" gaps, typ.

H

M L

A

1⅝" end gaps

A

I I I

H

F

G

G

17⅝"

17⅝"

B

B

FRONT VIEW

5⅞"

3 1/16"

1⅞" rad.

17¼"

2¾"

17½"

BACK LEGS

1½"

3/4" rad.

C

80°

K

J

5/16" gaps, typ.

K

D

A

B

12½"

E

3"

SIDE VIEW

32½" rad.

D & G

SEAT SUPPORTS & BRACES

PHOTO A: Lay out and cut the back legs. A band saw works best for making uniform cuts in thick stock, like this mahogany. Feed the workpieces slowly through the blade, steering from both the side and the back to follow your layout lines.

PHOTO B: When all the pieces of the leg assemblies have been cut, shaped and sanded, position the parts and dry-clamp them together. Draw pairs of short lines across each joint to mark for drilling dowel holes.

This bench is built entirely of Honduras mahogany, a very dense, finely-grained wood that has excellent natural durability in outdoor settings and needs no finish. In order to get 1¾-in.-thick stock for this project, you'll likely have to buy 8/4 (2-in.) stock and plane it down to final thickness.

BUILD THE LEG ASSEMBLIES

❶ Make the back legs. Refer to the *Back Legs* drawing, page 151, to draw the back leg profiles onto 1¾-in. mahogany stock. Cut out the legs on your band saw (**See Photo A**). Sand the cut edges.

❷ Make the arm rests. Cut blanks to length and width. Bevel-cut the back ends to 10° and cut the top front corners to a ¾-in. radius. Rout a ¼-in. roundover on the top edges of the arms using a router and roundover bit.

❸ Make the seat supports. Again, cut the blanks to length and width from 1¾-in. stock. Then mark the 32½-in.-radius arc on the top of the blanks with trammel points or a string compass, and cut out the profiles on a band saw.

❹ Cut the front legs and end stretchers to length and width.

❺ Mark the dowel locations. Lay the parts for the leg assemblies in place on a worksurface and clamp them together. Mark pairs of dowel hole locations across each joint to use as drilling references **(See Photo B)**.

❻ Drill the dowel holes. Note that the dowels in the end stretchers are smaller than the others ($5/16 \times 1\frac{1}{2}$ in.), because the proportions of these stretchers are smaller. Use a doweling jig as a guide **(See Photo C)**, and drill the holes $\frac{1}{8}$ in. deeper than necessary in order to provide a little clearspace in the ends of the holes for glue.

❼ Build the leg assemblies. Set aside the arms, which will be attached later. Insert glue-coated fluted dowels into the ends of the seat supports and the end stretchers. Drop a generous spot of glue into the dowel holes in the legs, and spread a thin layer of glue onto the mating surfaces of the wood. Clamp up both leg assemblies **(See Photo D)**, using wood cauls to protect the leg surfaces from being marred by the clamps.

BUILD THE SEAT ASSEMBLY

❽ Make the stretchers and braces. Cut all the pieces to length, then mark the $32\frac{1}{2}$-in.-radius arc profiles on the braces and cut with a band saw. Sand the cuts smooth.

❾ Mark and drill the $\frac{3}{8}$-in.-dia. dowel holes. On the stretchers, mark the centerlines of the brace positions using the *Front View* drawing, page 151. Mark centerlines on the ends of the braces as well, from edge to edge. Mark matching dowel locations on the ends of the braces and the inside faces of the stretchers. Use a doweling jig to drill the pilot holes.

PHOTO C: Disassemble the clamped-up leg assemblies and extend the dowel reference lines across the ends of the workpieces. Drill holes with a doweling jig. Mark the bit depth with tape.

PHOTO D: Insert glue-covered dowels into the seat supports and stretchers, then coat the ends of the mating parts with glue and assemble the leg assemblies. Pull the joints tight with clamps.

PHOTO E: With the dowel joints of the braces and stretchers glued up, clamp the seat assembly and check for square by measuring the diagonals. Adjust as needed by repositioning the clamps.

PHOTO F: With a ¾-in.-wide dado blade installed on your table saw, set the height to ¾ in. and machine a groove, end to end, into one edge of both back rails. These will be the channels that accept the back slats and spacer blocks.

PHOTO G: A power miter saw makes quick work of cutting the back slats to a consistent length. Clamp a stopblock to the saw fence 13¼ in. from the blade, and cut the slats.

⑩ Build the seat assembly. Spread glue on the dowels and insert them into the braces. Spread glue onto the mating wood surfaces as well. Fit the stretchers and braces together, and clamp up the assembly. Before the glue sets, check the seat for square **(See Photo E)** by measuring corner-to-corner. If the diagonals are not equal, the assembly is out of square. Realign the parts by adjusting the clamps.

BUILD THE BACK ASSEMBLY
⑪ Make the back rails. Cut the rails to length from 1¾-in. stock. Set up your table saw with a dado blade, and cut a ¾ × ¾-in. groove down the center of one edge of both rails **(See Photo F)** to accept the back slats and spacers.

⑫ Make the back slats. Rip the slat stock to width on the table saw. Then clamp a stopblock to the fence of a power miter saw and use it as an index to crosscut all the slats to exactly the same length **(See Photo G)**.

⑬ Make the short spacers. Rip a piece of ¾ × ¾-in. stock at least 6 ft. long. Crosscut the short spacers to length on the miter saw.

⑭ Install the slats and spacers in the bottom rail. It works best to start with the center slat and work toward the ends; this way, even if there are slight discrepancies in lengths of spacers or widths of slats, the end spaces will be equal and the slats will be accurately centered in the completed back assembly. Begin by measuring and marking the centerlines on the faces of the top and bottom rails. Stand the bottom rail on its edge, and lay a bead of wood glue along the bottom and sides of the groove. Apply a light coat of glue around the end of the center slat, and insert it into the groove at the center of the rail. Apply glue to the surfaces of two spacers, position one on each side of the first slat, and tack them in position with pin nails or finish nails. If you hammer the nails rather than install them with a pneumatic nail gun, recess the nailheads with a nailset. Install the remaining slats and spacers similarly (**See Photo H**). When you come to the end of the rails, measure, cut and insert the four long spacers.

15 Install the top rail. Lay a bead of glue onto the bottom and sides of the rail's groove. Position the rail over the ends of the slats and clamp lightly in place so you can still adjust the slats slightly if needed. Apply glue to the spacers and insert them between the slats (**See Photo I**), tacking them in place with nails. After all the spacers have been installed, check the back assembly for square. Clamp the assembly until the glue dries.

16 Clean up any dried glue that squeezed out of the joints with a sharp chisel.

ASSEMBLE THE BENCH

17 Drill dowel holes for connecting the three subassemblies—legs, seat and back. Refer to the *Side View* drawing, page 151, for orienting the back and seat on the leg assemblies. Drill pairs of 3/8-in.-dia. holes for dowels to connect the back rails and seat stretchers to the bench legs. Dry-fit the bench together with dowels to check the fit of the parts. Then disassemble the subassemblies.

18 Make the seat slats. Cut the inner and outer slats to length, and ease the edges on one face of each slat with a router and 1/4-in.

PHOTO H: Locate the position of the center seat slat in the bottom rail. Working from the middle toward each end, secure the slats and short spacers in the bottom rail with glue. Nail the spacers in place. We used a pneumatic nail gun and pin nails.

PHOTO I: Attach the top rail to the back assembly by applying glue along the three inside faces of the rail's groove and clamping. Install spacer blocks between the slats on this rail as well.

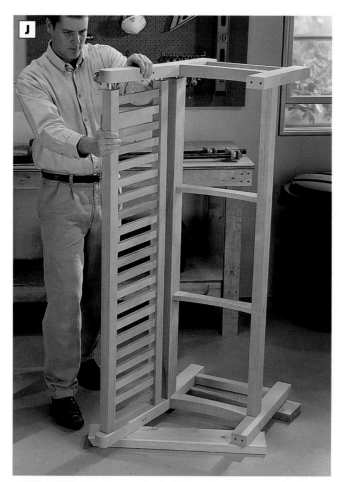

PHOTO J: After the rear seat slat has been attached, lay a leg assembly on the floor and set the back and seat into position. Then set the other leg assembly in place. Use glue and dowels in all the joints.

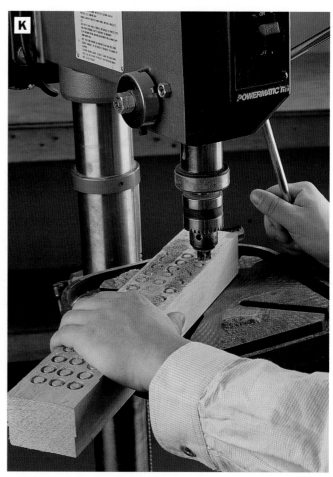

PHOTO K: Mount a ³⁄₈-in. plug cutter in your drill press to cut wood plugs for the screws. Cut about 56 plugs into the face grain of a length of mahogany. Bore the plug cutter ¹⁄₂ in. deep into the wood.

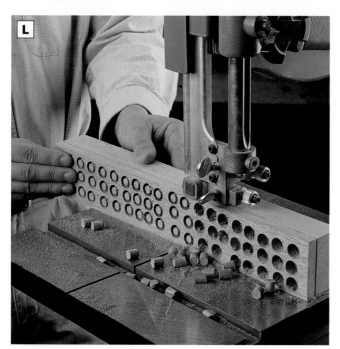

PHOTO L: Trim all the plugs to ⁷⁄₁₆ in. long in one operation by cutting along the face of the plug area using a band saw. Doing so will release the plugs.

roundover bit. Measure and mark the centerlines of the attachment screws. Drill pilot holes along the guidelines that are counterbored ³⁄₈ in., in order to install wood plugs above the screw heads.

19 Attach the rear slat to the back stretcher of the seat assembly. Install it so the front edge of the slat is flush with the inside edge of the back seat stretcher. This slat needs to be fastened now before the back assembly is installed. Otherwise the back will obstruct drill/driver access to drill and install screws.

20 Assemble the bench. Lay one end assembly on the floor. Put a spot of glue in the dowel holes. Insert glue-coated, fluted dowels into the ends of the back rails and seat stretchers, spread a thin layer of glue onto the mating surfaces of the joints, and position the back and seat on the end assembly. Apply glue to the remaining dowels and insert them into the other end of the rails and stretchers. Slip the other end assembly in place (**See Photo J**), and clamp the bench structure together.

21 Attach the remaining seat slats. Fasten the slats in place with countersunk 1½-in. flathead wood screws. Use a ⁵⁄₁₆-in. spacer to ensure uniform gaps between the inner slats.

22 Cut the screw plugs. You'll need approximately 56 wood plugs. Make them by mounting a plug cutter in your drill press and boring into the face grain of a single piece of mahogany stock (**See Photo K**). After boring for the plugs, cut along the mahogany slab ⁷⁄₁₆ in. in from the board's face with a band saw to cut the plugs free (**See Photo L**).

23 Install the plugs with glue, using a small brush. Insert plugs into the counterbores and seat them by tapping gently with a wooden mallet. When the glue dries, trim the plugs with a flush-cutting saw (**See Photo M**) and sand the plug areas smooth.

24 Attach the arm rest to the arm assembly. Insert glue-coated dowels into the arm rest, apply a thin layer of glue to the mating surfaces of the wood, and install the arm rests (**See Photo N**).

FINISHING TOUCHES

25 Go over the entire bench with sandpaper to smooth all surfaces.

26 You may apply UV protectant sealer if desired. However, Honduras mahogany is usually left unfinished, as it weathers to a soft gray color that blends with natural garden settings.

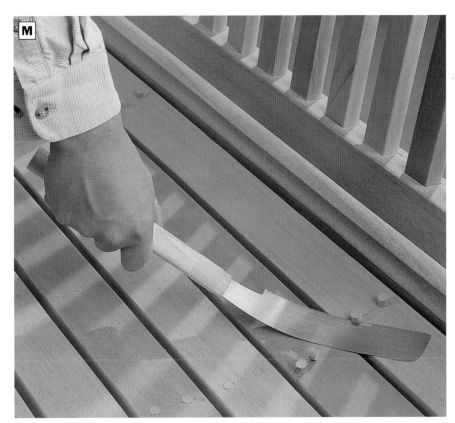

PHOTO M: After the glue dries, trim the plugs with a flush-cutting saw. Given the cup in the seat, use a flexible blade saw that can adjust to the contour of the slats. Be careful not to mar the seat slats as you trim against them.

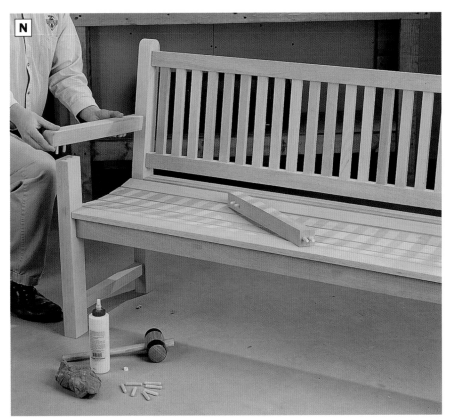

PHOTO N: Glue dowels into holes drilled previously in the arm rest. Coat the mating surfaces with glue, then attach the arm rests to the end assemblies and tap into place with a wooden mallet.

Index

Index of Projects